The Weekend Small Business Start-Up Kit

(+CD-ROM)

Mark Warda
Attorney at Law

SPHINX® PUBLISHING
AN IMPRINT OF SOURCEBOOKS, INC.®
NAPERVILLE, ILLINOIS
www.SphinxLegal.com

First Edition: 2007

Published by: **Sphinx® Publishing, An Imprint of Sourcebooks, Inc.®**

Naperville Office
P.O. Box 4410
Naperville, Illinois 60567-4410
630-961-3900
Fax: 630-961-2168
www.sourcebooks.com
www.SphinxLegal.com

This publication is designed to provide accurate and authoritative information in regard to the subject matter covered. It is sold with the understanding that the publisher is not engaged in rendering legal, accounting, or other professional service. If legal advice or other expert assistance is required, the services of a competent professional person should be sought.

From a Declaration of Principles Jointly Adopted by a Committee of the
American Bar Association and a Committee of Publishers and Associations

This product is not a substitute for legal advice.

Disclaimer required by Texas statutes.

Library of Congress Cataloging-in-Publication Data
Warda, Mark.
  The weekend small business start-up kit : (+CD-ROM) / by Mark Warda.
-- 1st ed.
      p. cm.
  Includes index.
  ISBN-13: 978-1-57248-603-4 (pbk. : alk. paper)
  ISBN-10: 1-57248-603-1 (pbk. : alk. paper)
  1. Small business--Law and legislation--United States--Popular works.
  2. New business enterprises--Law and legislation--United
States--Popular works. I. Title.

KF1659.Z9W37 2006
346.73'0652--dc22
                                                                2007012994

Printed and bound in the United States of America.
SB — 10 9 8 7 6 5 4 3 2 1

Contents

Know Your Strengths
Know Your Business
Sources for Further Guidance

Basic Forms of Doing Business
Start-Up Procedures
Foreign Nationals

Searching a Name
Fictitious Names
Sample Fictitious Name Notice
Corporate Names
Professional Associations
The Word *Limited*
Trademarks
Domain Names

How to Use the CD-ROM

Thank you for purchasing *The Weekend Small Business Start-Up Kit*. In this book, we have worked hard to compile exactly what you need to start your small business quickly, so that you can start making money. To make this material even more useful, we have included every document in the book on the CD-ROM in the back of the book.

You can use these forms just as you would the forms in the book. Print them out, fill them in, and use them however you need. You can also fill in the forms directly on your computer. Just identify the form you need, open it, click on the space where the information should go, and input your information. Customize each form for your particular needs. Use them over and over again.

The CD-ROM is compatible with both PC and Mac operating systems. (While it should work with either operating system, we cannot guarantee that it will work with your particular system and we cannot provide technical assistance.) To use the forms on your computer, you will need to use Microsoft Word or another word processing program that can read Word files. The CD-ROM does not contain any such program.

Insert the CD-ROM into your computer. Double-click on the icon representing the disc on your desktop or go through your hard drive to identify the drive that contains the disc and click on it.

Once opened, you will see the files contained on the CD-ROM listed as "Form #: [Form Title]." Open the file you need. You may print the form to fill it out manually at this point, or you can click on the appropriate line to fill it in using your computer.

Any time you see bracketed information [ ] on the form, you can click on it and delete the bracketed information from your final form. This information is only a reference guide to assist you in filling in the forms and should be removed from your final version. Once all your information is filled in, you can print your filled-in form.

*   *   *   *   *

Purchasers of this book are granted a license to use the forms contained in it for their own personal use. By purchasing this book, you have also purchased a limited license to use all forms on the accompanying CD-ROM. The license limits you to personal use only and all other copyright laws must be adhered to. No claim of copyright is made in any government form reproduced in the book or on the CD-ROM. You are free to modify the forms and tailor them to your specific situation.

The author and publisher have attempted to provide the most current and up-to-date information available. However, the courts, Congress, and your state's legislatures review, modify, and change laws on an ongoing basis, as well as create new laws from time to time. Due to the very nature of the information and the continual changes in our legal system, to be sure that you have the current and best information for your situation, you should consult a local attorney or research the current laws yourself.

This publication is designed to provide accurate and authoritative information in regard to the subject matter covered. It is sold with the understanding that the publisher is not engaged in rendering legal, accounting, or other professional service. If legal advice or other expert assistance is required, the services of a competent professional person should be sought.

—From a Declaration of Principles Jointly Adopted by a Committee of the American Bar Association and a Committee of Publishers and Associations

This product is not a substitute for legal advice.

—Disclaimer required by Texas statutes

Introduction

Small businesses are booming! The best way to take part in this boom is to run your own business.

This book is intended to give you the framework for legally opening your own small business.

In order to cover all of the aspects of any business you are thinking of starting, you should read through this entire book, rather than skipping to the parts that look most interesting. Many start-up items that may not sound like they apply to you do have provisions that will affect your business.

DISCLAIMER:

This book provides an introduction to starting a business anywhere in the United States. However, it is very important to note that every state has its own laws regarding every stage of setting up and running a business, and these state laws are often stricter than federal law. Be sure to use the resources in the appendices, as well as online tools like www.findlaw.com, to research your state's laws and comply with them.

Chapter 1:

Deciding to Start a Business

If you are reading this book, then you have probably made a serious decision to take the plunge and start your own business. Hundreds of thousands of people make the same decision each year, and many of them become very successful. A lot of them also fail. Knowledge can only help your chances of success. You need to know why some businesses succeed while others fail. Some of what follows may seem obvious, but to someone wrapped up in a new business idea, some of this information is occasionally overlooked.

Know Your Strengths

The last thing a budding entrepreneur wants to hear is that he or she is not cut out for running a business. You might avoid those "do you have what it takes" quizzes because you are not sure you want hear the answer. However, you can be successful if you know where to get the skills you lack.

You should consider all of the skills and knowledge that running a successful business requires, and decide whether you have what it takes. If you do not, it does not necessarily mean you are doomed to be an employee all your life. Perhaps you just need a partner who has the skills you lack. Perhaps you can hire someone with the skills you need, or you can structure your business to avoid areas where you are weak. If those tactics do not work, maybe you can learn the skills.

For example, if managing employees is not your strong suit, you can:

- handle product development yourself, and have a partner or manager deal with employees;
- take seminars in employee management; or,
- structure your business so that you do not need employees (use independent contractors or set yourself up as an independent contractor).

When planning your business, consider the following factors.

- *If it takes months or years before your business turns a profit, do you have the resources to hold out?* Businesses have gone under or have been sold just before they were about to take off. Staying power is an important ingredient to success.
- *Are you willing to put in a lot of overtime to make your business a success?* Owners of businesses do not set their own hours—the business sets hours for the owner. Many business owners work long hours seven days a week. You have to enjoy running your business and be willing to make some personal time sacrifices.
- *Are you willing to do the dirtiest or most unpleasant work of the business?* Emergencies come up and employees are not always dependable. You might need to mop up a flooded room, spend a weekend stuffing 10,000 envelopes, or work Christmas if someone calls in sick.
- *Do you know enough about the product or service?* Are you aware of the trends in the industry and what changes new technology might bring? Think of the people who started typesetting or printing businesses just before type was replaced by laser printers.
- *Do you know enough about accounting and inventory to manage the business?* Do you have a good head for business? Some people naturally know how to save money and do things profitably. Others are in the habit of buying the best or the most expensive of everything. The latter can be fatal to a struggling new business.
- *Are you good at managing employees?* If your business has employees (or will have in the future), managing them is an unavoidable part of running the business.

◆ *Do you know how to sell your product or service?* You can have the best product on the market, but people will not know about it unless you tell them about it. If you are a wholesaler, shelf space in major stores is hard to get, especially for a new company without a record, a large line of products, or a large advertising budget.

◆ *Do you know enough about getting publicity?* The media receives thousands of press releases and announcements each day, and most are thrown away. Do not count on free publicity to put your name in front of the public.

Know Your Business

Not only do you need to know the concept of a business, but you need the experience of working in a business. Maybe you have always dreamed of running a bed and breakfast or having your own pizza place. Have you ever worked in such a business? If not, you may have no idea of the day-to-day headaches and problems of the business. For example, do you really know how much to allow for theft, spoilage, and unhappy customers?

You might feel silly taking an entry-level job at a pizza place when you would rather start your own, but it might be the most valuable preparation you do. A few weeks of seeing how a business operates could mean the difference between success and failure.

Working in a business as an employee is one of the best ways to be a success at running such a business. People with new ideas can revolutionize established industries with obvious improvements that no one before dared to try.

Sources for Further Guidance

There are many things to consider as you prepare to start your own business. Most likely, you will have numerous questions that need to be answered before opening your doors for the first time. Luckily, there are many resources available for help. The sources discussed in this section offer free or low-cost guidance for new businesses.

SCORE

The Service Corps of Retired Executives (SCORE) is a resource partner with the U.S. Small Business Administration (SBA). It is the premier source for free and confidential small business advice for entrepreneurs. SCORE is dedicated to entrepreneurial education and the formation, growth, and success of small businesses nationwide.

SCORE is a 501(c)(3) nonprofit organization that offers small business advice and training nationwide through 10,500 volunteer counselors. The counselors are working or retired business owners, executives, and corporate leaders who share their wisdom and lessons learned in business. SCORE mentors entrepreneurs through one-to-one business advising sessions on a full range of business topics. There are numerous SCORE locations, and a location near you can be found by visiting their website at **www.score.org**. You can meet with counselors one-on-one and attend local workshops. You can even ask questions online. SCORE has helped over 7.5 million small businesses succeed.

Small Business Development Centers

The U.S. Small Business Administration (SBA) administers the Small Business Development Center Program (SBDCs) to provide management assistance to current and prospective small business owners. These centers offer one-stop assistance to individuals and small businesses by providing a wide variety of information and guidance in central and easily accessible branch locations.

The program is a cooperative effort of the private sector, the educational community, and federal, state, and local governments. An SBDC can be found in every state, and there are more than 1,100 service locations throughout the country. The service locations are located at colleges, universities, community colleges, vocational schools, chambers of commerce, and economic development corporations. The assistance you receive will be tailored toward your individual needs and the community in which you operate. Visit **www.sba.gov/sbdc** for more information.

Other Offices

The Small Business Administration offers many other programs and services throughout the country. In addition to the free counseling, advice, and information on starting a business through SCORE, and free consulting services and training events (some require a nominal registration fee) through the network of SBDCs, the SBA offers:

- financial assistance for new or existing businesses through guaranteed loans made by area bank and non-bank lenders;
- assistance to businesses owned and controlled by socially and economically disadvantaged individuals through the Minority Enterprise Development Program;
- advice to women business owners through Women's Business Ownership Representatives;
- special loan programs for businesses involved in international trade; and,
- guaranteed loans for creditworthy veterans.

You can find a full array of the programs the SBA offers on its website at **www.sba.gov**. The SBA's website is a great resource for any new small business and should definitely be checked out before you get started, and also all along your way.

Chapter 2:

Choosing the Form of Your Business

Before starting your business, you should choose the form of your business. That is, you should choose whether you will do business in your own name, with a partner, or as a legal entity such as a corporation or LLC. Forming and maintaining an artificial entity is usually not particularly expensive and generally considered well worth the cost in terms of the protection against liability it provides. However, depending on your venture, formalizing your business may not be necessary. Still, you should make sure you consider the advantages and disadvantages of your decision.

Basic Forms of Doing Business

The five most common forms for a small business are proprietorship, partnership, limited partnership, corporation, and limited liability company. The characteristics, advantages, and disadvantages of each are discussed in this section.

Proprietorship

A *proprietorship* is one person doing business in his or her own name or under a fictitious name.

Advantages. Simplicity is a proprietorship's greatest advantage. There is also no organizational expense, and no extra tax forms or reports to file.

Disadvantages. The proprietor is personally liable for all debts and obligations. There is also no continuation of the business after death. All profits are directly taxable, which is certainly a disadvantage for the proprietor, and business affairs are easily mixed with personal affairs.

General Partnership

A *general partnership* involves two or more people carrying on a business together to share the profits and losses.

Advantages. Partners can combine expertise and assets. A general partnership allows liability to be spread among more persons. Also, the business can be continued after the death of a partner if it is bought out by a surviving partner.

Disadvantages. Each partner is liable for acts of other partners within the scope of the business. This means that if your partner harms a customer or signs a million-dollar credit line in the partnership's name, you can be personally liable. Also, even if you leave all profits in the business, those profits are taxable. Control is shared by all parties, and the death of a partner may result in liquidation. In a general partnership, it is often hard to get rid of a bad partner.

Limited Partnership

A *limited partnership* has characteristics similar to both a corporation and a partnership. There are general partners who have the control and personal liability, and there are limited partners who only put up money and whose liability is limited to what they paid for their share of the partnership (like corporate stock). A new type of limited partnership, a *limited liability limited partnership*, allows all partners to avoid liability.

Advantages. Capital can be contributed by limited partners who have no control of the business or liability for its debts.

Disadvantages. A great disadvantage to a limited partnership is high start-up costs. Also, an extensive partnership agreement is required because general partners are personally liable for partnership debts and for the acts of each other. (One solution to this problem is to use a corporation as the general partner.)

Corporation

A *corporation* is an artificial legal "person" that carries on business through its officers for its shareholders. This legal person carries on business in its own name, and shareholders are not necessarily liable for its acts. In many states, one person may form a corporation and be its sole shareholder and officer.

An *S corporation* is a corporation that has filed Internal Revenue Service (IRS) **FORM 2553 ELECTION BY A SMALL BUSINESS CORPORATION**, thus choosing to have all profits taxed to the shareholders, rather than to the corporation. An S corporation files a tax return, but pays no federal or state tax. The profit shown on the S corporation tax return is reported on the owners' tax returns.

A *C corporation* is any corporation that has not elected to be taxed as an S corporation. A C corporation pays income tax on its profits. The effect of this is that when dividends are paid to shareholders, they are taxed twice—once for the corporation and once when they are paid to the shareholders. A C corporation may also have to pay corporate income tax to the state in which it is incorporated or authorized to do business.

A *professional service corporation* is a corporation formed by professionals, such as doctors or accountants. Most states have special rules for professional service corporations that differ slightly from those of other corporations. The department that oversees corporations in your state, usually the secretary of state, will often have these rules available for you online.

A *nonprofit corporation* is usually used for organizations such as religious groups and condominium associations. However, with careful planning, some types of businesses can be set up as nonprofit corporations and save a lot in taxes. While a nonprofit corporation cannot pay dividends, it can pay its officers and employees fair salaries. Some of the major American nonprofit organizations pay their officers well over $100,000 a year.

Advantages. If a corporation is properly organized, shareholders have no liability for corporate debts and lawsuits, and officers usually have no personal liability for their corporate acts. The existence of a corporation may be perpetual. There are tax advantages allowed only to corporations. There is prestige in owning a corporation. Two of the most important advantages to doing business as a corporation are the ability to raise capital by issuing stock and the ease of transferring ownership upon death.

A small corporation can be set up as an S corporation to avoid corporate taxes, but still retain corporate advantages. Some types of businesses can be set up as nonprofit corporations that provide significant tax savings.

Disadvantages. The start-up costs for forming a corporation are certainly a disadvantage. Plus, there are certain formalities to comply with, such as annual meetings, separate bank accounts, and more complicated tax forms. Unless a corporation registers as an S corporation, it must pay federal income tax separate from the tax paid by the owners, and must pay United States income tax. Over the years, there have occasionally been proposals to tax S corporations with an exemption for small operations, but none have passed the legislature.

Limited Liability Company

A *limited liability company* (LLC) is like a limited partnership without general partners. It has characteristics of both a corporation and a partnership—none of the partners have liability and all can have some control.

Advantages. The limited liability company offers the tax benefits of a partnership with the protection from liability of a corporation. While both a corporation and an LLC offer a business owner protection from business debts, the LLC also offers protection of the company's assets from the debts of an owner. It offers more tax benefits than an S corporation, because it may pass through more depreciation and deductions, have different classes of ownership, have an unlimited number of members, and have aliens as members. It is similar to a Latin-American *Limitada* or a German *GmbH*.

Disadvantages. An LLC that is set up as a disregarded entity might pay more Social Security taxes on business income than a S corporation. This can be eliminated by opting to be taxed as an S corporation.

Start-Up Procedures

Unless you are setting up as a sole proprietorship, you must prepare some paperwork to start your business, and for some types, you must file the paperwork and pay a registration fee.

Proprietorship

In a proprietorship, all accounts, property, and licenses are taken in the name of the owner. See Chapter 3 for a discussion of fictitious names.

Partnership

To form a partnership, a written agreement should be prepared to spell out the rights and obligations of the parties. It may be registered with the secretary of state, but this is not required. Most accounts, property, and licenses can be in either the partnership name or the partners' names.

Limited Partnership

A written *limited partnership agreement* must be drawn up and registered with your secretary of state, and a lengthy disclosure document given to all prospective limited partners. Because of the complexity of securities laws and the criminal penalties for violation, it is advantageous to have an attorney organize a limited partnership.

Corporation

To form a corporation, *articles of incorporation* (sometimes called a *charter* or *certificate of incorporation*) must be filed with the secretary of state (or the governmental agency in your state where articles are filed), along with the proper filing fees. An organizational meeting is then held. At the meeting, officers are elected, stock is issued, and other formalities are complied with in order to avoid the corporate entity being set aside later and treated as though it was never formed. Licenses and accounts are titled in the name of the corporation. One person or more may form a for-profit corporation, but at least three persons are needed to form a nonprofit corporation.

Limited Liability Corporation

One or more persons may form a limited liability company by filing *articles of organization* with the secretary of state (or the governmental agency in your state where articles are filed). Licenses and accounts are titled in the name of the company.

Foreign Nationals

Persons who are not citizens or legal permanent residents of the United States are typically free to start any type of business organization. The type that would be most advantageous would be the LLC, because federal tax law allows it to have foreign owners (unlike an S corporation) and it avoids corporate taxation (unlike a C corporation).

Two legal issues that foreign persons should be concerned with when starting a business are their immigration status and the proper reporting of the business's foreign owners. The ownership of a U.S. business does not automatically confer rights to enter or remain in the United States. Different types of visas are available to investors and business owners, and each of these has strict requirements.

A visa to enter the United States may be permanent or temporary. Permanent visas for business owners usually require investments to be from $500,000 to $1,000,000 and to result in the creation of new jobs. However, there are ways to obtain visas for smaller investments, if structured right. For more information on this area, consult an immigration specialist or a book on immigration.

Temporary visas may be used by business owners to enter the United States. However, these are hard to get, because in most cases, the foreign person must prove that there are no U.S. residents qualified to take the job.

Reporting

Businesses in the U.S. that own real property and are controlled by foreigners are required to file certain federal reports under the *International Investment Survey Act*, the *Agricultural Foreign Investment Disclosure Act*, and the *Foreign Investment in Real Property Tax Act* (FIRPTA). If these laws apply to your business, you should consult an attorney who specializes in foreign ownership of U.S. businesses.

Chapter 3:

Naming Your Business

Before deciding upon a name for your business, you should be sure that it is not already being used by someone else. Many business owners have spent thousands of dollars on publicity and printing, only to throw it all away because another company owned the name. A company that owns a name can take you to court and force you to stop using that name. It can also sue you for damages if it thinks your use of the name cost it a financial loss.

Even if you will be running a small local shop with no plans for expansion, you should at least check out whether the name has been trademarked. If someone else is using the same name anywhere in the country and has registered it as a federal trademark, they can sue you if you use it. If you plan to expand or to deal nationally, then you should do a thorough search of the name.

Searching a Name

Once you have chosen the perfect name, you need to be sure that no one else has established legal rights to it. Legal rights can be established by registering a name as a trademark or by merely using the name. Consequently, you cannot be sure no one has rights to a name just by checking registered names. You need to check if anyone is using the name but has not yet registered it.

The following are places you should check.

Federal Trademarks

First, you should check if anyone has registered the name as a federal trademark. To be sure that your use of the name does not violate someone else's trademark rights, you should have a trademark search done of the mark in the *United States Patent and Trademark Office* (PTO). In the past, this required a visit to their offices or the hiring of a search firm for over $100. However, now this can be done on the Internet by going to the United States Patent and Trademark Office website (**www.uspto.gov**) and clicking the "Search" button under "Trademarks."

Yellow Pages

Search the Yellow Page listings next. With Internet access, you can search all of the Yellow Page listings in the U.S. at a number of sites at no charge. One website, **www.superpages.com**, offers free searches of Yellow Pages for all states at once. You can also use a search engine, such as **www.google.com**, to see if your company name is used anywhere on the Internet. Since search engines are not always 100% accurate, you should search on at least a few other sites for the state in which you will operate.

Web Addresses

If you have any expectation of having a website some day, you should check if the Web address, or *uniform resource locator* (URL), is available. This can be done at **www.domainname.com**.

Search Services

If you are unable to access the Internet in any way or if you would rather have someone else do the search, you can hire a professional search firm. In addition to a trademark search, they can check other records around the country to give you a more accurate answer as to whether the name is being used anywhere. The cost can range from about $100 to over $800, depending on how thorough the search is and who is doing it. The following are a few firms that do searches. You can call or write to them for a quote.

Government Liaison Services, Inc.
200 North Glebe Road
Suite 321
Arlington, VA 22203
800-624-6564
703-524-8200
Fax: 703-525-8451
www.trademarkinfo.com

Thomson & Thomson
500 Victory Road
North Quincy, MA 02171
800-692-8833
Fax: 800-543-1983
www.thomson-thomson.com

Blumberg Excelsior Corporate Services, Inc.
4435 Old Winter Garden Road
P.O. Box 2122
Orlando, FL 32802
800-327-9220
407-299-8220
Fax: 407-291-6912
www.blumberg.com

Secretary of State

Finally, you should check with the secretary of state in the state in which you plan to register your corporation to see if the name is available. In some states, this can be done over the phone or on the Internet. In others, you must send a written inquiry.

No matter how thorough your search is, there is no guarantee that there is not a local user somewhere with rights to the mark. If, for example, you register a name and later find out that someone in Tucumcari, New Mexico has been using the name longer than you, that person will still have the right to use the name, but just in his or her local area.

The best way to make sure a name you are using is not already owned by someone else is to make one up. Names such as Xerox, Kodak, and Exxon were made up and did not have any meaning prior to their use. Remember that there are millions of businesses, and even something you make up may already be in use. Do a search just to be sure.

Fictitious Names

In most states, unless you do business in your own legal name, you must register the name you are using, called a *fictitious name*. When you use a fictitious name, you are *doing business as* (d/b/a) whatever name you are using. The name must be registered with your secretary of state's office, or depending on your state's procedure, with the county in which you will be doing business. When doing your name search, you should be sure to check the county records as well as with the state, so you do not run into issues down the road.

Requirements and Exemptions

Registering your fictitious name is very important. In some states, it is a misdemeanor to fail to register a fictitious name, and you may not sue anyone unless you are registered. If someone sues you and you are not registered, you may have to pay their attorney's fees and court costs.

If your name is John Doe and you are operating a masonry business, you may operate your business as "John Doe, Mason" without registering it. However, any other use of a name should be registered, such as:

Doe Masonry	Doe Masonry Company
Doe Company	Florida Sunshine Masonry

Legally, you would use the full name "John Doe d/b/a Doe Masonry."

You cannot use the words "corporation," "incorporated," "corp.," or "inc." unless you are a corporation. However, corporations do not have to register the name they are using unless it is different from their registered corporate name. (See "Corporate Names" on p.18 for more information on this subject.)

Obtaining a Fictitious Name

To register a fictitious name, you must first place an ad announcing your intent to use the name. Place the ad in a newspaper of general circulation for the county in which you will be maintaining your principal place of business. The ad must generally run from one to three times over as many weeks. If you were in Florida, for example, the ad would typically be placed in the classified section under "Legal Notices" and could be worded as follows.

FICTITIOUS NAME NOTICE

Notice is hereby given that the undersigned, desiring to engage in business under the name of DOE COMPANY, intend to register the name with the Clerk of the Circuit Court of Liberty County, Florida.

JOHN DOE   75% Owner

JIM DOE   25% Owner

John Doe, 123 Main Street, Libertyville, FL 32101

You should compare ad rates before placing the ad. Many counties have weekly newspapers that specialize in legal ads and charge a third of what the large newspapers charge. Check the newsstands, especially around the courthouse.

After the ad has appeared, you must file an Application for Registration of Fictitious Name or similarly named document with the secretary of state or county department in charge of registration. Unlike corporate names and trademarks, fictitious name registrations are accepted without regard to who else is using the name. Registration of a fictitious name does not bestow any rights to the name upon the registrant—it merely notifies the world of who is behind the business. Anyone can register any name, even if a hundred others have already registered that name.

As discussed previously, you should do some research to see if the name you intend to use is already being used by anyone else. Even persons who have not registered a name can acquire some legal rights to the name through mere use.

Corporate Names

A corporation does not have to register a fictitious name because it already has a legal name. The name of a corporation must contain one of the following words:

Incorporated	Inc.
Corporation	Corp.
Company	Co.

It is not advisable to use only the word "Company" or "Co.," because unincorporated businesses also use these words, and a person dealing with you might therefore not realize you are incorporated. If this happens, you might end up with personal liability for corporate debts. You may use a combination of two of the words, such as "ABC Co., Inc."

If the name of the corporation does not contain one of the above words, it will be rejected by the secretary of state. It will also be rejected if the name is already taken, if it is similar to the name of another corporation, or if it uses a forbidden word such as "Bank" or "Trust." Most secretary of states' website's have online name checking sections where you can see if the corporate name you want to use is available.

If a name you pick is taken by another company, you may be able to change it slightly and have it accepted. For example, if there is already a Tri-City Upholstery, Inc., and it is in a different county, you may be allowed to use "Tri-City Upholstery of Liberty County, Inc." However, even if this is approved by the secretary of state, you might get sued by the other company if your business is close to theirs or there is a likelihood of confusion. Do not have anything printed with your business name on it until you have final approval.

If a corporation wants to do business under a name other than its corporate name, it can register a fictitious name, such as "Doe Corporation d/b/a Doe Industries." However, if the name leads people to believe that the business is not a corporation, the right to limited liability may be lost. If you use such a name, it should always be accompanied by the corporate name.

Professional Associations

Professionals such as attorneys, doctors, dentists, life insurance agents, and architects can form corporations or limited liability companies in which to practice. These are better than general partnerships because they protect the professional from the malpractice of his or her coworkers.

In most states, a professional corporation cannot use the usual corporate designations (Inc., Corp., or Co.), but must use the designations "Professional Association," "P.A.," or "Chartered." Some states use abbreviations such as P.C. (professional corporation) or P.S.C. (professional service corporation). Check with your secretary of state to see what is required in your state.

A professional LLC can use "chartered," "professional limited company," "P.L.," or "L.C."

The Word *Limited*

The word *limited* or the abbreviation *ltd.* should not be used unless the entity is a limited partnership or limited liability company. If a corporation wishes to use the word *limited* in its name, it must still use one of the corporate words or abbreviations, such as *incorporated* or *corp.*

Trademarks

As your business builds goodwill, its name will become more valuable and you will want to protect it from others who may wish to copy it. To protect a name used to describe your goods or services, you can register it as a *trademark* (for goods) or a *service mark* (for services) with either your secretary of state or with the United States Patent and Trademark Office (or both).

You cannot obtain a trademark for the name of your business, but you can trademark the name you use on your goods and services. In most cases, you use your company name on your goods as your trademark. In effect, it protects your company name. Another way to protect your company name is to incorporate. A particular corporate name can only be registered by one company in any particular state.

State registration would be useful if you only expect to use your trademark within your state. Federal registration would protect your mark anywhere in the country. The registration of a mark gives you exclusive use of the mark for the types of goods for which it is registered. The only exception is for people who have already been using the mark. You cannot stop people who have been using the mark prior to your registration.

Federal Registration

There are two types of applications for federal registration, depending upon whether you have already made *actual use* of the mark or whether you merely have an *intention to use* the mark in the future. For a trademark that has been in use, you must file an application form along with specimens showing actual use and a drawing of the mark that complies with all of the rules of the United States Patent and Trademark Office (PTO).

For goods, this means it must be used on the goods themselves, or on containers, tags, labels, or displays of the goods. For services, it must be used in the sale or advertising of the services. The use must be in an actual transaction with a customer. A sample mailed to a friend is not an acceptable use.

For an intent to use application, you must file two separate forms—one when you make the initial application and the other after you have made actual use of the mark—as well as the specimens and a drawing. Before a mark can be entitled to federal registration, the use of the mark must be in *interstate commerce*—commerce with another state. The fee for registration is $375, but if you file an intent-to-use application there is a second fee of $100 for the filing after actual use. To encourage electronic filing of trademark application, there are reduced fee options of $325 and $275 if you meet the minimum requirements and strict filing requirements respectively for electronic filing.

Domain Names

Once you have a valid trademark, you will be safe using it for your domain name. In recent years, several new *top-level domains* (TLDs) have been created. TLDs are the last letters of the URL (uniform resource locator), such as ".com," ".org,"and ".net." Now you can also register names with the following TLDs.

.biz	.pro
.cc	.aero
.info	.coop
.name	.museum

To find out if a domain name is available, go to **www.whois.net**.

Chapter 4:

Preparing a Business Plan

Not everyone needs a business plan to start a business, but if you have one it might help you avoid mistakes and make better decisions. For example, if you think it would be a great idea to start a candle shop in a little seaside resort, you might find out after preparing a business plan that considering the number of people who might stop by, you could never sell enough candles to pay the rent.

A business plan lets you look at the costs, expenses, and potential sales, and see whether or not your plan can be profitable. It also allows you to find alternatives that might be more profitable. In the candle shop example, you might find that if you chose a more populous location or if you sold something else in addition to the candles, you would be more likely to make a profit.

Advantages and Disadvantages of a Business Plan

Other than helping you figure out if your business will be profitable, a business plan would also be useful if you hope to borrow money or have investors buy into your business. Lenders and equity investors always require a business plan before they will provide money to a business.

On the other hand, if your idea is truly unusual, a business plan may discourage you from starting your business. A business idea might look like a failure on paper, but if in your gut you know it would work, it might be worth trying without a business plan.

Example: *When Chester Carlson invented the first photocopy machine, he went to IBM. They spent $50,000 to analyze the idea and concluded that nobody needed a photocopy machine because people already had carbon paper—which was cheaper. However, he believed in his machine and started Xerox Corporation, which became one of the biggest and hottest companies of its time.*

However, even with a great concept, you need to at least do some basic calculations to see if the business can make a profit.

◆ If you want to start a retail shop, figure out how many people are close enough to become customers and how many other stores will be competing for those customers. Visit some of those other shops and see how busy they are. Without giving away your plans to compete, ask some general questions like "how's business?" and maybe they will share their frustrations or successes.

◆ Whether you sell a good or a service, do the math to find out how much profit is in it. For example, if you plan to start a house painting company, find out what you will have to pay to hire painters, what it will cost you for all of the insurance, what bonding and licensing you will need, and what the advertising will cost you. Figure out how many jobs you can do per month and what other painters are charging. In some industries, there may be a large margin of profit in one area of the state, while in other areas there may be almost no profit.

◆ Find out if there is a demand for your product or service. Suppose you have designed a beautiful new kind of candle and your friends all say you should open a shop because "everyone will want them." Before making a hundred of them and renting a store, bring a few to craft shows or flea markets and see what happens.

◆ Figure out what the income and expenses would be for a typical month of your new business. List monthly expenses, such as rent, salaries, utilities, insurance, taxes, supplies, advertising, services, and other overhead. Then, figure out how much profit you will average from each sale. Next, figure out how many sales you will need to cover your overhead and divide by the number of business days in the month. Can you reasonably expect that many sales? How will you get those sales?

Most types of businesses have trade associations, which often have figures on how profitable its members are. Some even have start-up kits for people wanting to start businesses. One good source of information on such organizations is the *Encyclopedia of Associations,* published by Gale Research Inc., and available in many library reference sections. Suppliers of products to the trade often give assistance to small companies getting started, to win their loyalty. Contact the largest suppliers of the products your business will be using and see if they can be of help.

Outline for Your Business Plan

While you may believe that you do not need a business plan, conventional wisdom says you do and it only makes good business sense to have one. A typical business plan has sections that cover topics such as the following:

◆ executive summary;
◆ product or service;
◆ market;
◆ competition;
◆ marketing plan;
◆ production plan;
◆ organizational plan;
◆ financial projections;
◆ management team; and,
◆ risks.

The following is an explanation of each.

Executive Summary

The executive summary is an overview of what the business will be and why it is expected to be successful. If the business plan will be used to lure investors, this section is the most important, since many might not read any further if they are not impressed with the summary.

Product or Service

The product or service section is a detailed description of what you will be selling. You should describe what is different about it and why people would need it or want it.

Market

The market section should analyze who the potential buyers of your product or service are. Describe both the physical location of the customers and their demographics. For example, a bodybuilding gym would probably mostly appeal to males in the 18 to 40 age bracket in a ten- to twenty-mile radius, depending on the location.

If you will sell things from a retail shop, you might also want to sell from mail order catalogs or over the Internet if your local customer base would not be large enough to support the business. Describe what you will be doing for those ventures.

If you are manufacturing things, you should find out who the wholesalers and distributors are, and their terms. This information should also be included in this section.

Competition

Before opening your business, you should know who and where your competitors are. If you are opening an antique shop, you might want to be near other antique shops so more customers come by your place, since antiques are unique and do not really compete with other antiques. However, if you open a florist shop, you probably do not want to be near other florist shops since most florists sell similar products and a new shop would just dilute the customer base.

If you have a truly unique way of selling something, you might want to go near other similar businesses to grab their existing customer base and expand your market share. However, if they could easily copy your idea, you might not take away the business for long and could end up diluting the market for each business.

Marketing Plan

Many a business has closed just a few months after opening because not enough customers showed up. How do you expect customers to find out about your business? Even if you get a nice write-up in the local paper, not everyone reads the paper, many people do not read every page, and lots of people forget what they read.

Your marketing plan describes how you will advertise your business. List how much the advertising will cost, and describe how you expect people to respond to the advertising.

Production Plan

The production plan needs to address and answer questions such as the following.
- ◆ If you are manufacturing a product, do you know how you will be able to produce a large quantity of them?
- ◆ Do you know all the costs and the possible production problems that could come up?
- ◆ If Wal-Mart orders 100,000 of them, could you get them made in a reasonable time?

The production plan needs to anticipate the normal schedule you intend to use, as well as how to handle any changes, positive or negative, to that schedule.

If you are selling a service and will need employees to perform those services, your production plan should explain how you will recruit and train those employees.

Organizational Plan

If your business will be more than a mom and pop operation, what will the organizational plan be? How many employees will you need and who will supervise whom?

How much of the work will be done by employees and how much will be hired out to other businesses and independent contractors? Will you have a sales force? Will you need manufacturing employees? Will your accounting, website maintenance, and office cleaning and maintenance be contracted out or done by employees?

Financial Projections

Tying all the previously discussed topics together is what your financial plan will discuss. You should know how much rent, utilities, insurance, taxes, marketing, product costs, and wages for labor will cost you for the first year. Besides listing known, expected expenses, you should calculate your financial well-being under a number of different possible scenarios. Some of the questions to think about and answer will be, *How long would you be in business if you have very few customers the first few months?*, and *If Wal-Mart does order 100,000 of your products, could you afford to manufacture them, knowing you will not be paid for months?*

Management Team

If you will be seeking outside funding, you will need to list the experience and skills of the management of the business. Investors want to know that the people have experience and know what they are doing.

Risks

A good business plan weighs all the risks of the new enterprise. Is new technology in the works that will make the business obsolete? Would a rise in the price of a particular needed supply eliminate all your profits? What are the chances of a new competitor entering the market if you show some success, and what are you going to do about it? Part of your analysis should be to look at all of the possible things that could happen in the field you chose and to gauge the likelihood of success.

Gathering Information

Some of the sections of your business plan require a lot of research. People sometimes take years to prepare them. Today, the Internet puts a nearly infinite amount of information at your fingertips, but you might also want to do some personal research.

Sometimes the best way to get the feel for a business is to get a job in a similar business. At a minimum, you should visit similar businesses and perhaps sit outside of one, and see how many customers they have and how much business they do. There are startup guides for many types of businesses, which can be found at Amazon.com, your local bookstores, and library. Your local chamber of commerce, business development office, or SCORE office might also have materials to help you in your research.

Sample Business Plan

The following plan is one for a simple one-person business that will use its owner's assets to start. Of course, a larger business, or one that needs financing, will need a much longer and more detailed plan.

A website with sixty sample business plans and information on business plan software is **www.bplans.com**.

Executive Summary

This is the plan for a new business, Reardon Computer Repair, LLC by Henry Reardon, to be started locally and then expanded throughout the state and perhaps further if results indicate this is feasible.

The mission of Reardon Computer Repair (RCR) is to offer fast, affordable repairs to office and home computers. The objective is to become profitable within the first three months and to grow at a quick but manageable pace.

In order to offer customers the quickest service, RCR will rely on youthful computer whizzes who are students and have the time and expertise to provide the service. They will also have the flexibility to arrive quickly and the motivation to show off their expertise.

To reach customers, we will use limited advertising, but primarily the Internet and word of mouth from happy customers.

With nearly every business and family having several computers and lack of fast service currently available, it is expected this business could be successful quickly and could grow rapidly.

Product or Service

The company will offer computer repair services both at its shop and at customers' offices and homes. It will sell computer parts as necessary to complete the repairs and it will also carry upgrades, accessories, and peripherals, which will most likely be of value to customers needing repairs.

Market

The market would be nearly every business and family at every address in the city, state, and country, since today nearly everyone has a computer. Figures show nearly 250 million computers in use in America, and that number is expected to grow to over 300 million in five years.

The market for the initial shop would be a fifteen-mile radius, which is a reasonable driving distance for our employees. The population in that area is 300,000 people, which would mean 240,000 potential customers, based on the current level of 800 computers per 1,000 people.

The market would not include new computers, which typically come with a one-year guarantee. It would also not include people who bought extended guarantees.

The growth trend for the industry is 8–10% for the next decade.

Competition

The competition would be the authorized repair shops working with the computer manufacturers. While these have the advantage of being authorized, research and experience has shown that they are slow and do not meet customers' needs for immediate repairs.

There is one computer repair shop within a ten-mile radius of the proposed shop and two more within a twenty-five-mile radius. Average wait time for a dropped-off repair is one week. The two closest repair services offer no on-site repair. Shipping a computer to a dealer for repair takes one to two weeks. Most customers need their computer fixed within a day or two.

One potential source for competition would be from employees or former employees who are asked to work for customers "on the side" at a reduced rate. To discourage this, the company will have a contract with employees with a non-compete agreement that specifies that they will pay the company three times what they earn should they violate that agreement. Also, agreements with customers will include a clause that they have the option to hire away one of our employees for a one-time $2,000 fee.

Marketing Plan

The business will be marketed through networking, Internet marketing, advertising, and creative marketing.

Networking will be through the owner's contacts and local computer clubs and software stores. Some local retailers do not offer service and they have already indicated that they would promote a local business that could offer fast repairs.

A website would be linked to local businesses and community groups, and to major computer repair referral sites.

Advertising would include the Yellow Pages and local computer club newsletters. Studies have shown that newspaper and television advertising would be too expensive and not cost effective for this type of business.

Creative advertising would include vinyl lettering on the back window of the owner's vehicle.

Production Plan

The company will be selling computer parts and the services of computer technicians. The owner will supply most of the services in the beginning and then add student technicians as needed.

The parts will all be purchased ready-made from the manufacturers, except for cables, which can be made on an as-needed basis much cheaper than ready-made ones.

Employees

The employees will be students who are extremely knowledgeable about computers. Some would call them computer "geeks"—in a nice way. They have extensive knowledge of the workings of computers, have lots of free time, need money, and would love to show off how knowledgeable they are.

As students, they already have health insurance and do not need full-time work. They would be available as needed. The company would pay them $12 an hour plus mileage, which is more than any other jobs available to students, but is not cost prohibitive, considering the charge to customers of $50 per hour.

Financial Projections

The minimum charge for a service call will be $75 on-site and $50 in-shop, which will include one hour of service. The parts markup will be the industry standard of 20%. The average customer bill will be estimated to be $100, including labor and markup.

The labor cost is estimated to be $30 per call including time, taxes, insurance, and mileage. The owner will be estimated to handle 75% of the work the first six months and 50% the second six months.

Rent, utilities, insurance, taxes, and other fixed costs is estimated to be $3,000 per month.

Advertising and promotion expenses are expected to be $3,000 per month.
Estimated number of customers will be:

First three months: 10 per week
Second three months: 20 per week
Third three months: 35 per week
Fourth three months: 50 per week

Estimated monthly revenue:
First three months: $4,000
Second three months: $8,000
Third three months: $14,000
Fourth three months: $20,000

Monthly income and expense projection:

First three months:
   Income $4,000
   Labor $300
   Fixed costs $3,000
   Advertising $3,000
   Net $2,300 loss per month

Second 3 months:
   Income $8,000
   Labor $600
   Fixed costs $3,000
   Advertising $3,000
   Net $1,400 profit per month

Third 3 months:
   Income $14,000
   Labor $2,100
   Fixed costs $3,000
   Advertising $3,000
   Net $5,900 profit per month

Fourth 3 months:
   Income $20,000
   Labor $3,000
   Fixed costs $3,000
   Advertising $3,000
   Net $11,000 profit per month

Organization Plan

The business will start with the owner, Henry Reardon, and three students who are experts at computer repair and available as part-time workers on an as-needed basis.

The owner will manage the business and do as many repairs as are possible with the time remaining in the week.

One of the students, Peter Galt, will work after school in the shop, and the others, Dom Roark and Howard Taggert, are willing to work on an on-call basis, either at the shop or at customers' homes.

As business grows, the company will recruit more student employees through the school job placement offices and at computer clubs.

Management Team

The owner, Henry Reardon, will be the sole manager of the company. He will use the accounting services of his accountant, Dave Burton. The owner anticipates being able to supervise up to ten employees. When there are more than ten, the company will need a manager to take over scheduling and some other management functions.

Risks

Because the business does not require a lot of capital, there will be a low financial risk in the beginning. The biggest reason for failure would be an inability to get the word out that the company exists and can fill a need when it arises. For this reason, the most important task in the beginning will be marketing and promotion.

As the company grows, the risk will be that computers will need fewer repairs, become harder to repair, and become so cheap they are disposable. To guard against this possibility, the company will add computer consulting services as it grows so that it will always have something to offer computer owners.

Chapter 5:

Financing Your Business

The way to finance your business is determined by how fast you want your business to grow and how much risk of failure you are able to handle. Letting the business grow with its own income is the slowest but safest way to grow. Taking out a personal loan against your house to expand quickly is the fastest but riskiest way to grow.

Growing with Profits

Many successful businesses have started out with little money and used the profits to grow bigger and bigger. If you have another source of income to live on (such as a job or a spouse's job), you can plow all the income of your fledgling business into growth.

Some businesses start as hobbies or part-time ventures on the weekend while the entrepreneur holds down a full-time job. Many types of goods or service businesses can start this way. Even some multi-million dollar corporations, such as Apple Computer, started out this way.

This allows you to test your idea with little risk. If you find you are not good at running that type of business, or the time or location was not right for your idea, all you are out is the time you spent and your start-up capital.

However, a business can only grow so big from its own income. In many cases, as a business grows, it gets to a point where the orders are so big that money must be borrowed to produce the product to fill them. With this kind of order, there is the risk that if the customer cannot pay or goes bankrupt, the business will also go under. At such a point, a business owner should investigate the creditworthiness of the customer and weigh the risks. Some businesses have grown rapidly, some have gone under, and others have decided not to take the risk and stayed small. You can worry about that down the road.

Using Your Savings

If you have savings you can tap to get your business started, that is the best source. You will not have to pay high interest rates and you will not have to worry about paying someone back. This section discusses some options for using your own savings to start your business, and potential pitfalls for each.

Home Equity

If you have owned your home for several years, it is possible that the equity has grown substantially and you can get a second mortgage to finance your business. If you have been in the home for many years and have a good record of paying your bills, some lenders will make second mortgages that exceed the equity. Just remember, if your business fails, you may lose your house.

Retirement Accounts

Be careful about borrowing from your retirement savings. There are tax penalties for borrowing from or against certain types of retirement accounts. Also, your future financial security may be lost if your business does not succeed.

Having Too Much Money

It probably does not seem possible to have too much money with which to start a business, but many businesses have failed for that reason. With plenty of start-up capital available, a business owner does not need to watch expenses and can become wasteful. Employees get used to lavish spending. Once the money runs out and the business must run on its own earnings, it fails.

Starting with the bare minimum forces a business to watch its expenses and be frugal. It necessitates finding the least expensive solutions to problems that crop up and creative ways to be productive.

Borrowing Money

It is extremely tempting to look to others to get the money to start a business. The risk of failure is less worrisome and the pressure is lower, but that is a problem with borrowing. If it is others' money, you do not have quite the same incentive to succeed as you do if everything you own is on the line.

Actually, you should be even more concerned when using the money of others. Your reputation is at risk, and if you do not succeed, you probably will still have to pay back the loan.

Family

Depending on how much money your family can spare, it may be the most comfortable or most uncomfortable source of funds for you. If you have been assured a large inheritance and your parents have more funds than they need to live on, you may be able to borrow against your inheritance without worry. It will be your money anyway, and you need it much more now than you will ten or twenty years from now. If you lose it all, it is your own loss.

However, if you are asking your widowed mother to cash in a certificate of deposit she lives on to finance your get-rich-quick scheme, you should have second thoughts about it. Stop and consider all the real reasons your business might not take off and what your mother would do without the income.

Friends

Borrowing from friends is like borrowing from family members. If you know they have the funds available and could survive a loss, you may want to risk it, but if they would be loaning you their only resources, do not chance it.

Financial problems can be the worst thing for a relationship, whether it is a casual friendship or a long-term romantic involvement. Before you borrow from a friend, try to imagine what would happen if you could not pay it back and how you would feel if it caused the end of your relationship.

The ideal situation is if your friend were a co-venturer in your business and the burden would not be totally on you to see how the funds were spent. Still, realize that such a venture will put extra strain on the relationship.

Banks

In a way, a bank can be a more comfortable party from which to borrow, because you do not have a personal relationship with them as you do with a friend or family member. If you fail, they will write your loan off rather than disown you. However, a bank can also be the least comfortable party to borrow from because they will demand realistic projections (your business plan) and be on top of you to perform. If you do not meet their expectations, they may call your loan just when you need it most.

The best thing about a bank loan is that they will require you to do your homework. You must have plans that make sense to a banker. If they approve your loan, you know that your plans are at least reasonable.

Bank loans are not cheap or easy. You will be paying a good interest rate, and you will have to put up collateral. If your business does not have equipment or receivables, the bank may require you to put up your house and other personal property to guarantee the loan.

Banks are a little easier to deal with when you get a Small Business Administration (SBA) loan. That is because the SBA guarantees that it will pay the bank if you default on the loan. SBA loans are obtained through local bank branches.

Credit Cards

Borrowing against a credit card is one of the fastest growing ways of financing a business, but it can be one of the most expensive ways. The rates can go higher than 20%, although many cards offer lower rates. Some people are able to get numerous cards. Some successful businesses have used credit cards to get off the ground or to weather through a cash crunch, but if the business does not begin to generate the cash to make the payments, you could soon end up in bankruptcy. A good strategy is only to use credit cards for a long-term asset, like a computer, or for something that will quickly generate cash, like buying inventory to fill an order. Do not use credit cards to pay expenses that are not generating revenue.

Getting a Rich Partner

One of the best business combinations is a young entrepreneur with ideas and ambition, and a retired investor with business experience and money. Together, they can supply everything the business needs.

How to find such a partner? Be creative. You should have investigated the business you are starting and know others who have been in such businesses. Have any of them had partners retire over the last few years? Are any of the current partners planning to phase out of the business?

Selling Shares of Your Business

Silent investors are the best source of capital for your business. You retain full control of the business, and if it happens to fail, you have no obligation to them. Unfortunately, few silent investors are interested in a new business. It is only after you have proven your concept to be successful and built up a rather large enterprise that you will be able to attract such investors.

The most common way to obtain money from investors is to issue stock to them. For this, the best type of business entity is the corporation. It gives you almost unlimited flexibility in the number and kinds of shares of stock you can issue.

Understanding Securities Laws

There is one major problem with selling stock in your business, and that is all of the federal and state regulations with which you must comply. Both the state and federal governments have long and complicated laws dealing with the sales of securities. There are also hundreds of court cases attempting to explain what these laws mean. A thorough explanation of this area of law is obviously beyond the scope of this book.

Basically, *securities* have been held to exist in any case in which a person provides money to someone with the expectation that he or she will get a profit through the efforts of that person. This can apply to any situation where someone buys stock in, or makes a loan to, your business. What the laws require is disclosure of the risks involved, and in some cases, registration of the securities with the government. There are some exemptions, such as for small amounts of money and for limited numbers of investors.

Penalties for violation of securities laws are severe, including triple damages and prison terms. You should consult a specialist in securities laws before issuing any security. You can often get an introductory consultation at a reasonable rate to learn your options.

Using the Internet to Find Capital

The Internet can also be a great resource for finding and marketing to investors. However, before attempting to market your company's shares on the Internet, be sure to get an opinion from a securities lawyer or do some serious research into securities law. The immediate accessibility of the Internet makes it very easy for you to get ahead of yourself and unintentionally violate state and federal securities laws. The Internet contains a wealth of information that can be useful in finding sources of capital. The following sites may be helpful.

America's Business Funding Directory

www.businessfinance.com

Small Business Administration

www.sba.gov

Inc. Magazine

www.inc.com

NVST

www.nvst.com

The Capital Network

www.thecapitalnetwork.com

Chapter 6:

Locating Your Business

The right location for your business will be determined by what type of business it is and how fast you expect it to grow. For some types of businesses, the location will not be important to your success or failure—in others, it will be crucial.

Working Out of Your Home

Many small businesses get started out of the home. Chapter 7 discusses the legalities of home businesses. This section discusses the practicalities.

Starting a business out of your home can save you the rent, electricity, insurance, and other costs of setting up at another location. For some people this is ideal, and they can combine their home and work duties easily and efficiently. For other people it is a disaster. A spouse, children, neighbors, television, and household chores can be so distracting that no other work gets done.

Since residential rates are usually lower than business lines, many people use their residential telephone line or add a second residential line to conduct business. However, if you wish to be listed in the Yellow Pages, you will need to have a business line in your home. If you are running two or more types of businesses, you can probably add their names as additional listings on the original number and avoid paying for another business line.

You also should consider whether the type of business you are starting is compatible with a home office. For example, if your business mostly consists of calling clients, then the home may be an ideal place to run it. If your clients need to visit you, or you will need daily pickups and deliveries by truck, then the home may not be a good location. This is discussed in more detail in Chapter 7.

Choosing a Retail Site

For most types of retail stores, the location is of prime importance. Things to consider include how close it is to your potential customers, how visible it is to the public, and how easily accessible it is to both autos and pedestrians. The attractiveness and safety of the site should also be considered.

Location would be less important for a business that was the only one of its kind in the area. For example, if there was only one moped parts dealer or Armenian restaurant in a metropolitan area, people would have to come to wherever you are if they want your products or services. However, even with such businesses, keep in mind that there is competition. People who want moped parts can order them by mail and restaurant customers can choose another type of cuisine.

You should look up all the businesses similar to the one you plan to run in the phone book and mark them on a map. For some businesses, like a cleaners, you would want to be far from the others. However, for other businesses, like antique stores, you would want to be near the others. (Antique stores usually do not carry the same things, they do not compete, and people like to go to an antique district and visit all the shops.)

Choosing Office, Manufacturing, or Warehouse Space

If your business will be the type where customers will not come to you, then locating it near customers is not as much of a concern and you can probably save money by locating away from the high-traffic central business districts. However, you should consider the convenience for employees, and not locate in an area that would be unattractive to them or too far from where they would likely live.

For manufacturing or warehouse operations, you should consider your proximity to a post office, trucking company, or rail line. When several sites are available, you might consider which one has the earliest or most convenient pickup schedule for the carriers you plan to use.

Leasing a Site

A lease of space can be one of the biggest expenses of a small business, so you should do a lot of homework before signing one. There are a lot of terms in a commercial lease that can make or break your business. The most critical terms are discussed in the following pages.

Zoning

Before signing a lease, you should be sure that everything that your business will need to do is allowed by the zoning of the property. Check the city and county zoning regulations.

Restrictions

In some shopping centers, existing tenants have guarantees that other tenants do not compete with them. For example, if you plan to open a restaurant and bakery, you may be forbidden to sell carryout baked goods if the supermarket next door has a bakery and a noncompete clause.

Signs

Business signs are regulated by zoning laws, sign laws, and property restrictions. If you rent a hidden location with no possibility for adequate signage, your chances for success are less than with a more visible site or much larger sign.

ADA Compliance

The *Americans with Disabilities Act* (ADA) requires that reasonable accommodations be made to make businesses accessible to the disabled. When a business is remodeled, many more changes are required than if no remodeling is done. Be sure that the space you rent complies with the law, or that the landlord will be responsible for compliance. Be aware of the full costs you will bear.

Expansion

As your business grows, you may need to expand your space. The time to find out about your options is before you sign the lease. Perhaps you can take over adjoining units when those leases expire.

Renewal

Location is a key to success for some businesses. If you spend five years building up a clientele, you do not want someone to take over your locale at the end of your lease. Therefore, you should have a renewal clause on your lease. Usually, this allows an increase in rent based on inflation.

Guarantee

Most landlords of commercial space will not rent to a small corporation without a personal guarantee of the lease. This is a very risky thing for a new business owner to do. The lifetime rent on a long-term commercial lease can be hundreds of thousands of dollars, and if your business fails the last thing you want to do is be personally responsible for five years of rent.

Where space is scarce or a location is hot, a landlord can get the guarantees he or she demands, and there is nothing you can do about it (except perhaps set up an asset protection plan ahead of time). However, where several units are vacant or the commercial rental market is soft, often you can negotiate out of the personal guarantee. If the lease is for five years, maybe you can get away with a guarantee of just the first year.

Duty to Open

Some shopping centers have rules requiring all shops to be open certain hours. If you cannot afford to staff it the whole time required, or if you have religious or other reasons that make this a problem, you should negotiate it out of the lease or find another location.

Sublease

At some point, you may decide to sell your business, and in many cases the location is the most valuable aspect of it. For this reason, you should be sure that you have the right to either assign your lease or to sublease the property. If this is impossible, one way around a prohibition is to incorporate your business before signing the lease, and then when you sell the business, sell the stock. However, some lease clauses prohibit transfer of *any interest* in the business, so read the lease carefully.

Buying a Site

If you are experienced with owning rental property, you will probably be more inclined to buy a site for your business. If you have no experience with real estate, you should probably rent and not take on the extra cost and responsibility of property ownership.

One reason to buy your site is that you can build up equity. Rather than pay rent to a landlord, you can pay off a mortgage and eventually own the property.

Separating the Ownership

One risk in buying a business site is that if the business gets into financial trouble, the creditors may go after the building as well. For this reason, most people who buy a site for their business keep the ownership out of the business. For example, the business will be a corporation and the real estate will be owned personally by the owner or by a trust unrelated to the business.

Expansion

Before buying a site, you should consider the growth potential of your business. If it grows quickly, will you be able to expand at that site or will you have to move? Might the property next door be available for sale in the future if you need it? Can you get an option on it?

If the site is a good investment whether or not you have your business, then by all means buy it. However, if its main use is for your business, think twice.

Zoning

Some of the concerns when buying a site are the same as when renting. You will want to make sure that the zoning permits the type of business you wish to start, or that you can get a variance without a large expense or delay. Be aware that just because a business is now using the site does not mean that you can expand or remodel the business at that site. Check with the zoning department of your local government and find out exactly what is allowed.

Signs

Signs are another concern. Some cities have regulated signs and do not allow new or larger ones. Some businesses have used these laws to get publicity. A car dealer who was told to take down a large number of American flags on his lot filed a federal lawsuit and rallied the community behind him.

ADA Compliance

Compliance with the Americans with Disabilities Act (ADA) is another concern when buying a commercial building. Find out from the building department if the building is in compliance or what needs to be done to put it in compliance. If you remodel, the requirements may be more strict.

NOTE: *When dealing with public officials, keep in mind that they do not always know what the law is, or do not accurately explain it. They often try to intimidate people into doing things that are not required by law. Read the requirements yourself and question the officials if they seem to be interpreting it incorrectly. Seek legal advice if officials refuse to reexamine the law or move away from an erroneous position.*

On the other hand, consider that keeping them happy may be worth the price. If you are already doing something they have overlooked, do not make a big deal over a little thing they want changed, or they may subject you to a full inspection or audit.

Checking Governmental Regulations

When looking for a site for your business, you should investigate the different governmental regulations in your area. For example, a location just outside the city or county limits might have a lower licensing fee, a lower sales tax rate, and less strict sign requirements.

Chapter 7:

Licensing Your Business

The federal and state legislatures and local governments have an interest in protecting consumers from bad business practices. In order to ensure that consumers are protected from unscrupulous businesspeople and to require a minimum level of service to the public, the federal, state, and local governments have developed hundreds of licensing requirements that cover occupations and services ranging from attorneys to barbers to day care providers.

Occupational Licenses and Zoning

In many areas, county and city governments require you to obtain an occupational license. If you are in a city, you may need both a city and a county license. Businesses that do work in several cities, such as builders, must obtain a license from each city in which they do work. This does not have to be done until you actually begin a job in a particular city.

County occupational licenses can be obtained from the tax collector in the county courthouse. City licenses are usually available at city hall. Be sure to find out if zoning allows your type of business before buying or leasing property. The licensing departments will check the zoning before issuing your license.

If you will be preparing or serving food, you will need to check with the local health department to be sure that the premises comply with their regulations. In some areas, if food has been served on the premises in the past, there is no problem getting a license. If food has never been served on the premises, then the property must comply with all the newest regulations. This can be very costly.

Home Businesses

Problems occasionally arise when people attempt to start businesses in their homes. Small, newer businesses cannot afford to pay rent for commercial space, and cities often try to forbid business in residential areas. Getting a county occupational license or advertising a fictitious name often gives notice to the city that a business is being conducted in a residential area.

Some people avoid the problem by starting their businesses without occupational licenses, figuring that the penalties for not having a license (if they are caught) are less expensive than the cost of office space. Others get the county license and ignore the city rules. If a person regularly parks commercial trucks and equipment on his or her property, has delivery trucks coming and going, or has employee cars parked along the street, there will probably be complaints from neighbors and the city will probably take legal action. However, if a person's business consists merely of making phone calls out of the home and keeping supplies there, the problem may never become an issue.

If a problem does arise regarding a home business that does not disturb the neighbors, a good argument can be made that the zoning law that prohibits the business is unconstitutional. When zoning laws were first instituted, they were not meant to stop people from doing things in a residence that had historically been part of the life in a residence. Consider an artist. Should a zoning law prohibit a person from sitting at home and painting pictures? Does selling them for a living there make a difference? Can the government force the rental of commercial space just because the artist decides to sell the paintings?

Similar arguments can be made for many home businesses. For hundreds of years people performed income-producing activities in their homes. On the other hand, court battles with a city are expensive and probably not worth the effort for a small business. The best course of action is to keep a low profile. Using a post office box for the business is sometimes helpful in diverting attention away from the residence.

Federal Licenses

Few businesses require federal registration. If you are in any of the types of businesses in the following list, you should check with the federal agency connected with it.

- ◆ Radio or television stations or manufacturers of equipment emitting radio waves:

Federal Communications Commission
445 12th Street, SW
Washington, DC 20554
www.fcc.gov

- ◆ Manufacturers of alcohol, tobacco, or firearms:

Bureau of Alcohol, Tobacco, Firearms, and Explosives
Office of Public and Governmental Affairs
650 Massachusetts Avenue, NW
Room 8290
Washington, DC 20226
www.atf.treas.gov

- ◆ Securities brokers and providers of investment advice:

Securities and Exchange Commission
100 F Street, NW
Washington, DC 20546
www.sec.gov

- ◆ Manufacturers of drugs and processors of meat:

Food and Drug Administration
5600 Fishers Lane
Rockville, MD 20857
www.fda.gov

◆ Interstate carriers:

Surface Transportation Board
1925 K Street, NW
Washington, DC 20423
www.stb.dot.gov

◆ Exporters:

Bureau of Industry and Security
Department of Commerce
14th Street & Constitution Avenue, NW
Washington, DC 20230
www.bis.doc.gov

Chapter 8:

Contract Laws

As a business owner, you will need to know the basics of forming a simple contract for your transactions with both customers and vendors. There is a lot of misunderstanding about what the law is, and people may give you erroneous information. Relying on it can cost you money. This chapter gives you a quick overview of the principles that apply to your transactions and the pitfalls to avoid. If you face more complicated contract questions, you should consult a law library or an attorney familiar with small business law.

Traditional Contract Law

One of the first things taught in law school is that a contract is not legal unless three elements are present—offer, acceptance, and consideration. The rest of the semester dissects exactly what may be a valid offer, acceptance, and consideration. For your purposes, the important things to remember are as follows.

- ◆ If you make an offer to someone, it may result in a binding contract, even if you change your mind or find out it was a bad deal for you.
- ◆ Unless an offer is accepted and both parties agree to the same terms, there is no contract.
- ◆ A contract does not always have to be in writing. Some laws require certain contracts to be in writing, but as a general rule, an oral contract is legal. The problem is in proving that the contract existed.
- ◆ Without *consideration* (the exchange of something of value or mutual promises), there is not a valid contract.

Basic Contract Rules

Some of the most important contract rules for a business owner are as follows.

- *An advertisement is not an offer.* Suppose you put an ad in the newspaper offering "New IBM computers only $995," but there is a typo in the ad and it says $9.95. Can people come in and say "I accept, here's my $9.95," creating a legal contract? Fortunately, no. Courts have ruled that an ad is not an offer that a person can accept. It is an invitation to come in and make offers, which the business can accept or reject.

- *The same rule applies to the price tag on an item.* If someone switches price tags on your merchandise, or if you accidentally put the wrong price on it, you are not required by law to sell it at that price. However, many merchants honor a mistaken price, because refusing to do so would constitute bad will and probably lose a customer. If you intentionally put a lower price on an item, intending to require a buyer to pay a higher price, you may be in violation of *bait and switch* laws.

- *When a person makes an offer, several things may happen.* It may be accepted, creating a legal contract; it may be rejected; it may expire before it has been accepted; or, it may be withdrawn before acceptance. A contract may expire either by a date made in the offer ("This offer remains open until noon on January 29, 2009") or after a reasonable amount of time. What is reasonable is a legal question that a court must decide. If someone makes you an offer to sell goods, clearly you cannot come back five years later and accept. Can you accept a week later or a month later and create a legal contract? That depends on the type of goods and the circumstances.

- *A person accepting an offer cannot add any terms to it.* If you offer to sell a car for $1,000, and the other party says he or she accepts as long as you put new tires on it, there is no contract. An acceptance with changed terms is considered a rejection and a counteroffer.

- *When someone rejects your offer and makes a counteroffer, a contract can be created by your acceptance of the counteroffer.*

These rules can affect your business on a daily basis. Suppose you offer to sell something to one customer over the phone, and five minutes later another customer walks in and offers you more for it. To protect yourself, you should call the first customer and withdraw your offer before accepting the offer of the second customer. If the first customer accepts before you have withdrawn your offer, you may be sued if you have sold the item to the second customer.

Exceptions

There are a few exceptions to the basic rules of contracts. Some of the important exceptions you need to know are as follows.

- *Consent to a contract must be voluntary.* If it is made under a threat, the contract is not valid. If a business refuses to give a person's car back unless they pay $500 for changing the oil, the customer could probably sue and get the $500 back.

- *Contracts to do illegal acts or acts against public policy are not enforceable.* If an electrician signs a contract to put some wiring in a house that is not legal, the customer could probably not force him or her to do it, because the court would refuse to require an illegal act.

- *If either party to an offer dies, then the offer expires and cannot be accepted by the heirs.* If a painter is hired to paint a portrait, and dies before completing it, his wife cannot finish it and require payment. However, a corporation does not die, even if its owners die. If a corporation is hired to build a house and the owner of the corporation dies, the heirs may take over the corporation, finish the job, and require payment.

- *Contracts made under misrepresentation are not enforceable.* For example, if someone tells you a car has 35,000 miles on it and you later discover it has 135,000 miles, you may be able to rescind the contract for fraud and misrepresentation.

- *If there was a mutual mistake a contract may be rescinded.* For example, if both you and the seller thought the car had 35,000 miles on it and both relied on that assumption, the contract could be rescinded. However, if the seller knew the car has 135,000 miles on it, but you assumed it had 35,000 and did not ask, you probably could not rescind the contract.

Statutory Contract Law

The previous section discussed the basics of contract law and some of the additional rules for when a contract can be made unenforceable. These are not usually stated in the statutes, but are the legal principles decided by judges over the past hundreds of years. In recent times, the legislatures have made numerous exceptions to these principles. In most cases, these laws have been passed when the legislature felt that traditional law was not fair.

Statutes of Fraud

Statutes of fraud state when a contract must be in writing to be valid. Some people believe a contract is not valid unless it is in writing, but that is not so. Only those types of contracts mentioned in the statutes of fraud must be in writing. Of course, an oral contract is much harder to prove in court than one that is in writing. Each state has its own statutes of frauds and may contain slight variations, but in general, the following contracts must be in writing to be enforceable:

- ◆ sales of any interest in real estate;
- ◆ leases of real estate over one year;
- ◆ guarantees of debts of another person;
- ◆ sales of goods of $500 or more;
- ◆ agreements that take over one year to complete; and,
- ◆ sales of securities.

Due to the alleged unfair practices by some types of businesses, laws have been passed controlling the types of contracts they may use. Most notable among these are health clubs and door-to-door solicitations. The laws covering these businesses usually give the consumer a certain time to cancel the contract. These advertising and promotion laws are described in Chapter 13.

Preparing Your Contracts

Before you open your business, you should obtain or prepare the contracts or policies you will use in your business. In some businesses, such as a restaurant, you will not need much. Perhaps you will want a sign near the entrance stating, "shirt and shoes required" or "diners must be seated by 10:30 p.m."

However, if you are a building contractor or a similar business, you will need detailed contracts to use with your customers. If you do not clearly spell out your rights and obligations, you may end up in court and you could lose thousands of dollars in profits.

Of course, the best way to have an effective contract is to have an attorney experienced on the subject prepare one to meet the needs of your business. However, since this may be too expensive for your new operation, you may want to go elsewhere. Three sources for the contracts you will need are other businesses like yours, trade associations, and legal form books. You should obtain as many different contracts as possible, compare them, and decide which terms are most comfortable for you.

Chapter 9:

Insurance

There are few laws requiring you to have insurance, but if you do not have insurance you may face liability that may ruin your business. You should be aware of the types of insurance available and weigh the risks of a loss against the cost of a policy.

Be aware that there can be a wide range of prices and coverage in insurance policies. You should get at least three quotes from different insurance agents and ask each one to explain the benefits of his or her policy.

Workers' Compensation

In most states, if you have one or more employees, you must carry *workers' compensation* insurance. This particular insurance protects employers from the financial loss that could result should an employee injury him- or herself on the job. The insurance is a no-fault type of coverage, and pays the employee for an injury while taking away the employee's right to sue you. Benefits typically include medical expenses, death and dismemberment benefits, lost wages, and vocational rehabilitation.

In most states, you can meet your workers' compensation obligations by purchasing an insurance policy from an insurance company. The coverage and costs will differ from company to company so you should shop around, but the policies are fairly standardized. Five states require employers to get coverage exclusively through state-operated funds. Those states are North Dakota, Ohio, Washington, West Virginia, and Wyoming. If you are doing business in any of those states, you need to obtain coverage from the specified government agency.

Fourteen other states also maintain a state fund, but private insurers also have the right to provide coverage in the state. The states that offer employers a state fund as well as allowing private insurers to provide coverage include the following: Arizona, California, Colorado, Idaho, Maryland, Michigan, Minnesota, Montana, Nevada, New York, Oklahoma, Oregon, Pennsylvania, and Utah. In these states, check with both the state agency and private insurers to determine which can provide you the best coverage for your needs.

In Texas and New Jersey, you do not have to provide workers' compensation coverage under the law, but you are still liable under those states' workers' compensation laws for injured workers, so not purchasing coverage is not a good idea.

If you are working alone or in a partnership in which only partners are also workers, you may not be required to purchase workers' compensation coverage for yourself. Only when you have employees that are also not owners are you generally required to carry coverage. Be aware, though, that in many states who counts as an employee for workers' compensation purposes is very broad and may include someone you hire that for other purposes would be an independent contractor, but for workers' compensation coverage would be considered an employee. It is wise to require anyone you hire in an independent contractor capacity to prove they are covered by a workers' compensation policy.

To protect yourself from litigation, you may wish to carry workers' compensation insurance even if you are not required to have it. For low-risk occupations, it is not expensive. If you have such coverage, you are protected against potentially ruinous claims by employees or their heirs in case of accident or death.

For high-risk occupations, such as roofing, it can be very expensive—sometimes thirty to fifty cents for each dollar of payroll. For this reason, construction companies try all types of ways to become exempt from the requirement to carry workers' compensation, such as hiring independent contractors or only having a few employees who are also officers of the business. However, the requirements for the exemptions are strict. Anyone intending to obtain an exemption should first check with an attorney specializing in workers' compensation to be sure to do it right.

Failure to provide workers' compensation insurance when required is considered serious. It could result in fines, jail time, and an injunction against employing anyone. If a person is injured on a job, even if another employee caused it or the injured person contributed to his or her own injury, you may be required to pay for all resulting losses.

Liability Insurance

In most cases, you are not required to carry liability insurance, but failing to do so could be a business disaster and ruin you financially.

Liability insurance can be divided into two main areas—coverage for injuries on your premises and by your employees, and coverage for injuries caused by your products or services.

Coverage for the first type of injury is usually very reasonably priced. Injuries in your business or by your employees (such as an auto accident) are covered by standard premises or auto policies. However, coverage for injuries by products may be harder to find and more expensive. The current trend in liability cases is for juries to award extremely high judgments for accidents involving products that sometimes had little impact on the accidents.

Asset Protection

If insurance is unavailable or unaffordable, you can go without and use a corporation and other asset protection devices to protect yourself from liability. The best way to find out if insurance is available for your type of business is to check with other businesses. If there is a trade group for your industry, their newsletter or magazine may contain ads for insurers.

Umbrella Policy

As a business owner, you will be a more visible target for lawsuits than as an individual, even if there is little merit to them. Lawyers know that a nuisance suit is often settled for thousands of dollars. Because of your greater exposure, you should consider getting a *personal umbrella policy*. This is a policy that covers you for claims of up to a million—or even two or five million—dollars, and is very reasonably priced.

Hazard Insurance

One of the worst things that can happen to your business is a fire, flood, or other disaster. With lost customer lists, inventory, and equipment, many businesses have been forced to close after such a disaster.

The premium for *hazard insurance* is usually reasonable and could protect you from losing your business. You can even get business interruption insurance, which will cover your losses while your business is getting back on its feet.

Home Business Insurance

There is a special insurance problem for home businesses. Most homeowner and tenant insurance policies do not cover business activities. In fact, under some policies, you may be denied coverage if you use your home for a business.

If you merely use your home to make business phone calls and send letters, you will probably not have a problem and not need extra coverage. However, if you own equipment or have dedicated a portion of your home exclusively to the business, you could have a problem. Check with your insurance agent for the options that are available to you.

If your business is a sole proprietorship and you have, say, a computer that you use both personally and for your business, it would probably be covered under your homeowners policy. If you incorporated your business and bought the computer in the name of the corporation, coverage might be denied. If a computer is your main business asset, you could get a special insurance policy in the company name covering just the computer. One company that offers such a policy is Safeware, and you can call them at 800-800-1492 or visit **www.safeware.com**.

Automobile Insurance

If you or any of your employees will be using an automobile for business purposes, be sure that such use is covered. Sometimes, a policy may contain an exclusion for business use. Check to be sure your liability policy covers you if one of your employees causes an accident while running a business errand.

Health Insurance

While new businesses can rarely afford health insurance for their employees, the sooner they can obtain it, the better chance they will have to find and keep good employees. As a business owner, you will certainly need health insurance for yourself (unless you have a working spouse who can cover the family), and you can sometimes get a better rate if you purchase a small business package.

Employee Theft

If you fear employees may be able to steal from your business, you may want to have them *bonded*. This means that you pay an insurance company a premium to guarantee employees' honesty, and if they cheat you, the insurance company pays you damages. This can cover all existing and new employees.

Chapter 10:

Your Business and the Internet

The Internet has opened up a world of opportunities for businesses. It was not long ago that getting national visibility cost a fortune. Today, a business can set up a Web page for a few hundred dollars, and with some clever publicity and a little luck, millions of people around the world will see it.

This new world has new legal issues and new liabilities. Not all of them have been addressed by laws or by the courts. Before you begin doing business on the Internet, you should know the existing rules and the areas where legal issues exist.

Domain Names

A *domain name* is the address of your website. For example, www.apple.com is the domain name of Apple Computer Company. The last part of the domain name, the ".com" (or "dot com") is the *top-level domain*, or TLD. Dot com is the most popular TLD, but others are currently available in the United States, including .net and .org. (Originally, .net was only available to network service providers and .org only to nonprofit organizations, but regulations have eliminated those requirements.)

It may seem like most words have been taken as a dot-com name, but if you combine two or three short words or abbreviations, a nearly unlimited number of possibilities are available. For example, if you have a business dealing with automobiles, most likely someone has already registered automobile.com and auto.com. You can come up with all kinds of variations, using adjectives or your name, depending on your type of business:

autos4u.com	joesauto.com	autobob.com
myauto.com	yourauto.com	onlyautos.com
greatauto.com	autosfirst.com	usautos.com
greatautos.com	firstautoworld.com	4autos.com

When the Internet first began, some individuals realized that major corporations would soon want to register their names. Since the registration was easy and cheap, people registered names they thought would ultimately be used by someone else.

At first, some companies paid high fees to buy their names from the registrants. One company, Intermatic, filed a lawsuit instead of paying. The owner of the domain name they wanted had registered numerous domain names, such as britishairways.com and ussteel.com. The court ruled that since Intermatic owned a trademark on the name, the registration of their name by someone else violated that trademark, and that Intermatic was entitled to it.

Since then, people have registered names that are not trademarks, such as CalRipkin.com, and have attempted to charge the individuals with those names to buy their domain. In 1998, Congress passed the *Anti-Cybersquatting Consumer Protection Act*, making it illegal to register a domain with no legitimate need to use it.

This law helped a lot of companies protect their names, but then some companies started abusing it and tried to stop legitimate users of names similar to theirs. This is especially likely against small companies. An organization that has been set up to help small companies protect their domains is the *Domain Name Rights Coalition*. Its website is **www.netpolicy.com**. Some other good information on domain names can be found at **www.bitlaw.com/internet/domain.html**.

Registering a domain name for your own business is a simple process. There are many companies that offer registration services. For a list of those companies, visit the site of the *Internet Corporation for Assigned Names and Numbers* (ICANN) at **www.icann.org**. You can link directly to any member's site and compare the costs and registration procedures required for the different top-level domains.

Web Pages

There are many new companies eager to help you set up a website. Some offer turnkey sites for a low, flat rate, while custom sites can cost tens of thousands of dollars. If you have plenty of capital, you may want to have your site handled by one of these professionals. However, setting up a website is a fairly simple process, and once you learn the basics, you can handle most of it in-house.

If you are new to the Web, you may want to look at **www.learnthenet.com** and **www.webopedia.com**, which will familiarize you with the Internet jargon and give you a basic introduction to the Web.

Site Setup

There are seven steps to setting up a website: site purpose, design, content, structure, programming, testing, and publicity. Whether you do it yourself, hire a professional site designer, or employ a college student, the steps toward creating an effective site are the same.

Before beginning your own site, you should look at other sites, including those of major corporations and of small businesses. Look at the sites of all the companies that compete with you. Look at hundreds of sites and click through them to see how they work (or do not work).

Site purpose. To know what to include on your site, you must decide what its purpose will be. Do you want to take orders for your products or services, attract new employees, give away samples, or show off your company headquarters? You might want to do several of these things.

Site design. After looking at other sites, you can see that there are numerous ways to design a site. It can be crowded, or open and airy; it can have several windows (frames) open at once or just one; and, it can allow long scrolling or just click-throughs.

You will have to decide whether the site will have text only; text plus photographs and graphics; or, text plus photos, graphics, and other design elements, such as animation or Java script. Additionally, you will begin to make decisions about colors, fonts, and the basic graphic appearance of the site.

Site content. You must create the content for your site. For this, you can use your existing promotional materials, new material just for the website, or a combination of the two. Whatever you choose, remember that the written material should be concise, free of errors, and easy for your target audience to read. Any graphics (including photographs) and written materials not created by you require permission. You should obtain such permission from the lawful copyright holder in order to use any copyrighted material. Once you know your site's purpose, look, and content, you can begin to piece the site together.

Site structure. You must decide how the content (text plus photographs, graphics, animation, etc.) will be structured—what content will be on which page, and how a user will link from one part of the site to another. For example, your first page may have the business name and then choices to click on, such as "about us," "opportunities," or "product catalog." Have those choices connect to another page containing the detailed information, so that a user will see the catalog when he or she clicks on "product catalog." Your site could also have an option to click on a link to another website related to yours.

Site programming and setup. When you know nothing about setting up a website, it can seem like a daunting task that will require an expert. However, *programming* here means merely putting a site together. There are inexpensive computer programs available that make it very simple.

Commercial programs such as Microsoft FrontPage, Dreamweaver, Pagemaker, Photoshop, MS Publisher, and PageMill allow you to set up Web pages as easily as laying out a print publication. These programs will convert the text and graphics you create into HTML, the programming language of the Web. Before you choose Web design software and design your site, you should determine which Web hosting service you will use. Make sure that the design software you use is compatible with the host server's system. The Web host is the provider who will give you space on their server and who may provide other services to you, such as secure order processing and analysis of your site to see who is visiting and linking to it.

If you have an America Online (AOL) account, you can download design software and a tutorial for free. You do not have to use AOL's design software in order to use this service. You are eligible to use this site whether you design your own pages, have someone else do the design work for you, or use AOL's templates. This service allows you to use your own domain name and choose the package that is appropriate for your business.

If you have used a page layout program, you can usually get a simple Web page up and running within a day or two. If you do not have much experience with a computer, you might consider hiring a college student to set up a Web page for you.

Site testing. Some of the website setup programs allow you to thoroughly check your new site to see if all the pictures are included and all the links are proper. There are also websites you can go to that will check out your site. Some even allow you to improve your site, such as by reducing the size of your graphics so they download faster. Use one other major search engines listed on page 72 to look for companies that can test your site before you launch it on the Web.

Site publicity. Once you set up your website, you will want to get people to look at it. *Publicity* means getting your site noticed as much as possible by drawing people to it.

The first thing to do to get noticed is to be sure your site is registered with as many *search engines* as possible. These are pages that people use to find things on the Internet, such as Yahoo and Google. They do not automatically know about you just because you created a website. You must tell them about your site, and they must examine and catalog it.

For a fee, there are services that will register your site with numerous search engines. If you are starting out on a shoestring, you can easily do it yourself. While there are hundreds of search engines, most people use a dozen or so of the bigger ones. If your site is in a niche area, such as genealogy services, then you would want to be listed on any specific genealogy search engines. Most businesses should be mainly concerned with getting on the biggest ones.

By far the biggest and most successful search engine today is Google (**www.google.com**). Some of the other big ones are:

www.altavista.com   www.lycos.com
www.excite.com   www.metacrawler.com
www.fastsearch.com   www.webcrawler.com
www.go.com   www.yahoo.com
www.hotbot.com

Most of these sites have a place to click to "add your site" to their system. Some sites charge hundreds of dollars to be listed. If your site contains valuable information that people are looking for, you should be able to do well without paying these fees.

Getting Your Site Known

A *meta tag* is an invisible subject word added to your site that can be found by a search engine. For example, if you are a pest control company, you may want to list all of the scientific names of the pests you control and all of the treatments you have available, but you may not need them to be part of the visual design of your site. List these words as meta tags when you set up your page so people searching for those words will find your site.

Some companies thought that a clever way to get viewers would be to use commonly searched names, or names of major competitors, as meta tags to attract people looking for those big companies. For example, a small delivery service that has nothing to do with UPS or FedEx might use those company names as meta tags so people looking for them would find the smaller company. While it may sound like a good idea, it has been declared illegal trademark infringement. Today many companies have computer programs scanning the Internet for improper use of their trademarks.

Once you have made sure that your site is passively listed in all the search engines, you may want to actively promote your site. However, self-promotion is seen as a bad thing on the Internet, especially if its purpose is to make money.

Newsgroups are places on the Internet where people interested in a specific topic can exchange information. For example, expectant mothers have a group where they can trade advice and experiences. If you have a product that would be great for expectant mothers, that would be a good place for it to be discussed. However, if you log into the group and merely announce your product, suggesting people order it from your website, you will probably be *flamed* (sent a lot of hate mail).

If you join the group, however, and become a regular, and in answer to someone's problem, mention that you "saw this product that might help," your information will be better received. It may seem unethical to plug your product without disclosing your interest, but this is a procedure used by many large companies. They hire *buzz agents* to plug their product all over the Internet and create positive *buzz* for the product. So, perhaps it has become an acceptable marketing method and consumers know to take plugs with a grain of salt. Let your conscience be your guide.

Keep in mind that Internet publicity works both ways. If you have a great product and people love it, you will get a lot of business. If you sell a shoddy product, give poor service, and do not keep your customers happy, bad publicity on the Internet can kill your business. Besides being an equalizer between large and small companies, the Internet can be a filtering mechanism between good and bad products.

Spamming

Sending unsolicited email advertising (*spam*) started out as a mere breach of Internet etiquette (netiquette) but has now become a state and federal crime. The ability to reach millions of people with advertising at virtually no cost was too good for too many businesses to pass up and this resulted in the clogging of most users' email boxes and near shutdown of some computer systems. Some people ended up with thousands of offers every day.

To prevent this, many states passed anti-spamming laws and Congress passed the CAN-SPAM Act. This law:

- ◆ bans misleading or false headers on email;
- ◆ bans misleading subject lines;
- ◆ requires allowing recipients to opt out of future mailings;
- ◆ requires the email be identified as advertising; and,
- ◆ requires the email include a valid physical address.

Each violation can result in up to an $11,000 fine and the fines can be raised if advertisers violate other rules such as not harvesting names and not using permutations of existing names. More information can be found on the Federal Trade Commission's website (**www.ftc.gov**).

Advertising

Advertising on the Internet has grown in recent years. At first, small, thin rectangular ads appeared at the top of websites; these are called *banner ads*. Lately they have grown bigger, can appear anywhere on the site, and usually blink or show a moving visual.

The fees can be based on how many people view an ad, how many click on it, or both. Some larger companies, such as Amazon.com, have affiliate programs in which they will pay a percentage of a purchase if a customer comes from your site to theirs and makes a purchase. For sites that have thousands of visitors the ads have been profitable—some sites reportedly make over $100,000 a year.

Example: *One financially successful site is Manolo's Shoe Blog (http://shoeblogs.com). It is written by a man who loves shoes, has a great sense of humor, and writes in endearing broken English. Because he is an expert in his field, his suggestions are taken by many readers who click through to the products and purchase them.*

Legal Issues

Before you set up a Web page, you should consider the many legal issues associated with websites.

Jurisdiction

Jurisdiction is the power of a court in a particular location to decide a particular case. Usually, you have to have been physically present in a jurisdiction or have done business there before you can be sued there. Since the Internet extends your business's ability to reach people in faraway places, there may be instances when you could be subject to legal jurisdiction far from your own state (or country). There are a number of cases that have been decided in this country regarding the Internet and jurisdiction, but very few cases have been decided on this issue outside of the United States.

In most instances, U.S. courts use the pre-Internet test—whether you have been present in another jurisdiction or have had enough contact with someone in the other jurisdiction. The fact that the Internet itself is not a "place" will not shield you from being sued in another state when you have shipped your company's product there, have entered into a contract with a resident of that state, or have defamed a foreign resident with content on your website.

According to the courts, there is a spectrum of contact required between you, your website, and consumers or audiences. (*Zippo Manufacturing Co. v. Zippo Dot Com, Inc.,* 952 F. Supp. 1119 (W.D. Pa 1997).) The more interactive your site is with consumers, the more you target an audience for your goods in a particular location, and the farther you reach to send your goods out into the world, the more it becomes possible for someone to sue you outside of your own jurisdiction—so weigh these risks against the benefits when constructing and promoting your website.

The law is not even remotely final on these issues. The American Bar Association, among other groups, is studying this topic in detail. At present, no final, global solution or agreement about jurisdictional issues with websites exists.

One way to protect yourself from the possibility of being sued in a faraway jurisdiction would be to state on your website that those using the site or doing business with you agree that "jurisdiction for any actions regarding this site" or your company will be in your home county.

For extra protection, you can have a preliminary page that must be clicked before entering your website. However, this may be overkill for a small business with little risk of lawsuits. If you are in any business for which you could have serious liability, you should review some competitors' sites and see how they handle the liability issue. They often have a place to click for "legal notice" or "disclaimer" on their first page.

You may want to consult with an attorney to discuss the specific disclaimer you will use on your website, where it should appear, and whether you will have users of your site actively agree to this disclaimer or just passively read it. However, these disclaimers are not enforceable everywhere in the world. Until there is global agreement on jurisdictional issues, this may remain an area of uncertainty for some time to come.

Libel

Libel is any publication that injures the reputation of another. This can occur in print, writing, pictures, or signs. All that is required for publication is that you transmit the material to at least one other person. When putting together your website, you must keep in mind that it is visible to millions of people all over the planet and that if you libel a person or company, you may have to pay damages.

Many countries do not have the freedom of speech that we do, and a statement that is not libel in the United States may be libelous elsewhere. If you are concerned about this, alter the content of your site or check with an attorney about libel laws in the country you think might take action against you.

Copyright Infringement

It is so easy to copy and borrow information on the Internet that it is easy to infringe copyrights without even knowing it. A *copyright* exists for a work as soon as the creator creates it. There is no need to register the copyright or to put a copyright notice on it. Therefore, practically everything on the Internet belongs to someone.

Some people freely give their works away. For example, many people have created Web artwork (*gifs* and *animated gifs*) that they freely allow people to copy. There are numerous sites that provide hundreds or thousands of free gifs that you can add to your Web pages. Some require you to acknowledge the source and some do not. You should always be sure that the works are free for the taking before using them.

Linking and Framing

One way to violate copyright laws is to improperly link other sites to yours, either directly or with framing. *Linking* is when you provide a link that takes the user to the linked site. *Framing* occurs when you set up your site so that when you link to another site, your site is still viewable as a frame around the linked-to site.

While many sites are glad to be linked to others, some, especially providers of valuable information, object. Courts have ruled that linking and framing can be a copyright violation. One rule that has developed is that it is usually okay to link to the first page of a site, but not to link to some valuable information deeper within the site. The rationale for this is that the owner of the site wants visitors to go through the various levels of their site (viewing all the ads) before getting the information. By linking directly to the information, you are giving away their product without the ads.

The problem with linking to the first page of a site is that it may be a tedious or difficult task to find the needed page from there. Many sites are poorly designed and make it nearly impossible to find anything.

If you wish to link to another page, the best solution is to ask permission. Email the webmaster or other person in charge of the site, if an email address is given, and explain what you want to do. If they grant permission, be sure to print out a copy of their email for your records.

Privacy

Since the Internet is such an easy way to share information, there are many concerns that it will cause a loss of individual privacy. The two main concerns arise when you post information that others consider private, and when you gather information from customers and use it in a way that violates their privacy.

While public actions of politicians and celebrities are fair game, details about their private lives are sometimes protected by law, and details about persons who are not public figures are often protected. The laws in each state are different, and what might be allowable in one state could be illegal in another. If your site will provide any personal information about individuals, you should discuss the possibility of liability with an attorney.

Several well-known companies have been in the news lately for violations of their customers' privacy. They either shared what the customer was buying or downloading, or looked for additional information on the customer's computer. To let customers know that you do not violate certain standards of privacy, you can subscribe to one of the privacy codes that have been created for the Internet. These allow you to put a symbol on your site guaranteeing to your customers that you follow the code.

The following are the websites of two organizations that offer this service and their fees at the time of this publication.

www.privacybot.com	$100
www.bbbonline.com	$200 to $7,000

Protecting Yourself

The easiest way to protect yourself personally from the various possible types of liability is to set up a corporation or limited liability company to own the website. This is not foolproof protection since, in some cases, you could be sued personally as well, but it is one level of protection.

COPPA

If your website is aimed at children under the age of thirteen, or if it attracts children of that age, and you collect any personal information, then you are subject to the federal *Children Online Privacy Protection Act of 1998* (COPPA). This law requires such websites to:

- ◆ give notice on the site of what information is being collected;
- ◆ obtain verifiable parental consent to collect the information;
- ◆ allow the parent to review the information collected;
- ◆ allow the parent to delete the child's information or to refuse to allow the use of the information;
- ◆ limit the information collected to only that necessary to participate on the site; and,
- ◆ protect the security and confidentiality of the information.

Hiring a Website Designer

If you hire someone to design your website, you should make sure of what rights you are buying. Under copyright law, when you hire someone to create a work, you do not get all rights to that work unless you clearly spell that out in a written agreement.

For example, if your designer creates an artistic design to go on your website, you may have to pay extra if you want to use the same design on your business cards or letterhead. Depending on how the agreement is worded you may even have to pay a yearly fee for the rights.

If you spend a lot of money promoting your business and a logo or design becomes important to your image, you would not want to have to pay royalties for the life of your business to someone who spent an hour or two putting together a design. Whenever you purchase a creative work from someone, be sure to get a written statement of what rights you are buying. If you are not receiving all rights for all uses for all time you should think twice about the purchase.

If the designer also is involved with hosting your site, you should be sure you have the right to take the design with you if you move to another host. You should get a backup of your site on a CD in case it is ever lost or you need to move it to another site.

Financial Transactions

When setting up your website, you should ask the provider if you can be set up with a secure site for transmitting credit card data. If they cannot provide it, you will need to contract with another software provider. Use one of the major search engines listed on page 72 to look for companies that provide credit card services to businesses on the Internet. Paypal is a very well known service, and Google has also launched a new payment service for Internet transactions.

As a practical matter, there is very little to worry about when sending credit card data by email. If you do not have a secure site, another option is to allow purchasers to fax or phone in their credit card data. However, keep in mind that this extra step will lose some business unless your products are unique and your buyers are very motivated.

The least effective option is to provide an order form on the site that can be printed out and mailed in with a check. Again, your customers must be really motivated or they will lose interest after finding out this extra work is involved.

FTC Rules

Because the Internet is an instrument of interstate commerce, it is a legitimate subject for federal regulation. The *Federal Trade Commission* (FTC) first said that all of its consumer protection rules applied to the Internet, but lately it has been adding specific rules and issuing publications. The following publications are available from the FTC website at **www.ftc.gov/bcp/menu-internet.htm** or by mail from:

Consumer Response Center
Federal Trade Commission
600 Pennsylvania, NW
Room H-130
Washington, DC 20580

- ◆ *Advertising and Marketing on the Internet: The Rules of the Road*
- ◆ *Appliance Labeling Rule Homepage*
- ◆ *BBB-Online: Code of Online Business Practices*
- ◆ *Big Print. Little Print. What's the Deal? How to Disclose the Details*
- ◆ *Businessperson's Guide to the Mail and Telephone Order Merchandise Rule*
- ◆ *CAN-SPAM Act: Requirements for Commercial Emailers*
- ◆ *Complying with the Telemarketing Sales Rule*
- ◆ *Disclosing Energy Efficiency Information: A Guide for Online Sellers of Appliances*
- ◆ *Dot Com Disclosures: Information About Online Advertising*
- ◆ *Electronic Commerce: Selling Internationally. A Guide for Business*
- ◆ *How to Comply With The Children's Online Privacy Protection Rule*
- ◆ *Frequently Asked Questions About the Children's Online Privacy Protection Rule*
- ◆ *Internet Auctions: A Guide for Buyer and Sellers*
- ◆ *"Remove Me" Responses and Responsibilities: Email Marketers Must Honor "Unsubscribe" Claims*
- ◆ *Securing Your Server—Shut the Door on Spam*
- ◆ *Security Check: Reducing Risks to Your Computer Systems*
- ◆ *Selling on the Internet: Prompt Delivery Rules*
- ◆ *TooLate.Com: The Lowdown on Late Internet Shipments*
- ◆ *Website Woes: Avoiding Web Service Scams*
- ◆ *What's Dot and What's Not: Domain Name Registration Scams*
- ◆ *You, Your Privacy Policy & COPPA*

Fraud

Because the Internet is somewhat anonymous, it is a tempting place for those with fraudulent schemes to look for victims. As a business consumer, you should exercise caution when dealing with unknown or anonymous parties on the Internet.

The U.S. Department of Justice, the FBI, and the National White Collar Crime Center jointly launched the *Internet Crime Complaint Center* (ICCC). If you suspect that you are the victim of fraud online, whether as a consumer or a business, you can report incidents to the ICCC on their website, **www.ic3.gov**. The ICCC is currently staffed by FBI agents and representatives of the National White Collar Crime Center, and will work with state and local law enforcement officials to prevent, investigate, and prosecute high-tech and economic crime online.

Chapter 11:

Health and Safety Laws

As a reaction to the terrible work conditions prevalent in the factories and mills of the nineteenth century industrial age, Congress and the states developed many laws intended to protect the health and safety of the nation's workers. These laws are difficult to understand and often seem to be very unfair to employers. Therefore, this is an area that you need to pay particular attention to as a new business. Failure to do so can result in terrible consequences for you.

OSHA

The federal government's laws regarding health and safety of workers are far-reaching and very important to consider in running your business, especially if you are a manufacturer or in the oil and gas, food production, or agriculture industries. Further, each state will have its own set of health and safety laws that you will need to look into depending on the type of business you plan to start.

The point of the *Occupational Safety and Health Administration* (OSHA) is to place the duty on the employer to keep the workplace free from recognized hazards that are likely to cause death or serious bodily injury to workers. The regulations are not as cumbersome for small businesses as for larger enterprises. If you have ten or fewer employees, or if you are in a certain type of business, you do not have to keep a record of illnesses, injuries, and exposure to hazardous substances of employees. If you have eleven or more employees, OSHA's rules will apply. One important rule to know is that within forty-eight hours of an on-the-job death of an employee or injury of five or more employees on the job, the area director of OSHA for your location must be contacted.

Visit their website, **www.osha.gov**, to obtain copies of their publications, *OSHA Handbook for Small Business* (OSHA 2209) and *OSHA Publications and Audiovisual Programs Catalog* (OSHA 2019). They also have a poster that is required to be a posted in the workplace. Find it at **www.osha.gov/Publications/poster.html**.

The *Hazard Communication Standard* requires that employees be made aware of the hazards in the workplace. (Code of Federal Regulations (C.F.R.), Title 29, Section (Sec.) 1910.1200.) It is especially applicable to those working with chemicals, but this can even include offices that use copy machines. Businesses using hazardous chemicals must have a comprehensive program for informing employees of the hazards and for protecting them from contamination.

For more information, you can contact OSHA at the previously mentioned addresses, phone numbers, or websites. They can supply a copy of the regulation and a booklet called *OSHA 3084,* which explains the law.

EPA

The *Worker Protection Standard for Agricultural Pesticides* requires safety training, decontamination sites, and of course, posters. The *Environmental Protection Agency* (EPA) will provide information on compliance with this law. They can be reached at 800-490-9198, or on their website at **www.epa.gov**.

FDA

The *Pure Food and Drug Act of 1906* prohibits the misbranding or adulteration of food and drugs. It also created the *Food and Drug Administration* (FDA), which has promulgated many regulations and which must give permission before a new drug can be introduced into the market. If you will be dealing with any food or drugs, you should keep abreast of their policies. Their website is **www.fda.gov**. The FDA's small business site is **www.fda.gov/ora/fed_state/small_ business**.

Hazardous Materials Transportation

There are regulations that control the shipping and packing of hazardous materials. For more information, contact:

Office of Hazardous Materials Safety
Research and Special Programs Administration
U.S. Department of Transportation
400 7ᵗʰ Street, SW
Washington, DC 20590

For an organizational structure of the Office of Hazardous Materials Safety and phone contacts, visit **http://hazmat.dot.gov/contact/org/org&ct.htm**.

CPSC

The *Consumer Product Safety Commission* (CPSC) has a set of rules that cover the safety of products. The commission feels that because its rules cover products, rather than people or companies, they apply to everyone producing such products. However, federal laws do not apply to small businesses that do not affect interstate commerce. Whether a small business would fall under a CPSC rule would depend on the size and nature of your business.

Search the CPSC's site at **www.cpsc.gov** for more information on these rules.

Additional Regulations

Every day there are proposals for new laws and regulations. It would be impossible to include every conceivable one in this book. To be up-to-date on the laws that affect your type of business, you should belong to a trade association for your industry and subscribe to newsletters that cover your industry. Attending industry conventions is a good way to learn more about federal regulations and to discover new ways to increase your profits.

Remember also that your state will have its own health and safety laws that you will need to be aware of and comply with.

Chapter 12:

Employment and Labor Laws

As they have with health and safety laws, Congress and the states have heavily regulated the actions that employers can take with regard to hiring and firing, improper employment practices, and discrimination. Because the penalties can be severe, educate yourself on the proper actions to take and consult a labor and employment lawyer, if necessary, prior to making important employee decisions.

Hiring and Firing Laws

For small businesses, there are not many rules regarding who you may hire or fire. The ancient law that an employee can be fired at any time (or may quit at any time) still prevails for small businesses. In certain situations and as you grow, however, you will come under a number of laws that affect your hiring and firing practices.

One of the most important things to consider when hiring someone is that if you fire him or her, that fired employee may be entitled to unemployment compensation. If so, your unemployment compensation tax rate will go up and it can cost you a lot of money. Therefore, you should only hire people you are sure you will keep, and you should avoid situations where your former employees can make claims against your company.

One way this can be done is by hiring only part-time employees. The drawback to this is that you may not be able to attract the best employees. When hiring dishwashers or busboys this may not be an issue, but when hiring someone to develop a software product, you do not want him or her to leave halfway through the development.

A better solution is to screen applicants to begin with and only hire those who you feel certain will work out. Of course, this is easier said than done. Some people interview well but then turn out to be incompetent at the job.

The best record to look for is someone who has stayed a long time at each of his or her previous jobs. Next best is someone who has not stayed as long (for good reasons), but has always been employed. The worst type of hire would be someone who is or has been collecting unemployment compensation.

The reason those who have collected compensation are a bad risk is that if they collect in the future, even if it is not your fault, your employment of them could make you chargeable for their claim. For example, you hire someone who has been on unemployment compensation and he or she works out well for a year, but then quits to take another job, and is fired after a few weeks. In this situation, you would be chargeable for most of his or her claim, because the last five quarters of work are analyzed in determining the amount of compensation. Look for a steady job history.

Often, the intelligence of an employee is more important than his or her experience. An employee with years of typing experience may be fast, but unable to figure out how to use your new computer, whereas an intelligent employee can learn the equipment quickly and eventually gain speed. Of course, common sense is important in all situations.

The bottom line is that you cannot know if an employee will be able to fill your needs from a résumé and interview. Once you have found someone who you think will work out, offer that person a job with a ninety-day probationary period. If you are not completely satisfied with the employee after the ninety days, offer to extend the probationary period for ninety additional days rather than end the relationship immediately. Of course, all of this should be in writing.

Employment Requirements

If you will be paying wages to anyone—even yourself—you will need to comply with all of the employer reporting and withholding laws of both your state and the federal government. The following is a summary of most of the requirements.

- ◆ *New hire reporting.* To improve the enforcement of child support payments, all employers must report the hiring of each new employee to an agency in the state.
- ◆ *Employment eligibility.* To combat the hiring of illegal immigrants, employers must complete the Department of Justice Form I-9 for each employee.
- ◆ *Federal tax withholding.* Social Security and income taxes must be withheld from employees' wages and deposited to an authorized bank quarterly, monthly, or more often, depending on the amount. The initial step is to obtain a Form W-4 from each employee upon hiring. (This same form can also be used to fulfill the new hire reporting law discussed above.)
- ◆ *State withholding.* In states that have income taxes, there is usually a withholding and reporting requirement similar to the federal one.
- ◆ *Local withholding.* In cities that have income taxes, there is usually a withholding and reporting requirement similar to the federal one.
- ◆ *Unemployment compensation.* Employers must pay taxes on employee wages to the state and federal governments regularly. Also, employers must submit reports both quarterly and annually.
- ◆ *Workers' compensation.* Depending on the number of employees and the type of work, the state may require that the employer obtain workers' compensation insurance.

Employees

There are many instances when you may need to hire people to help you get things accomplished. The hiring of an employee is a risky endeavor. As can be seen from the summary at the start of this section, there are numerous governmental laws and regulations that cover hiring, and failure to comply can result in financial penalties. For example, if someone does not have the legal right to work in this country, you can be fined for hiring him or her.

For these reasons, you should thoroughly check the background of anyone you hire. An **APPLICATION FOR EMPLOYMENT** can be used to get references and other information from a candidate. (See the CD-ROM for a blank version of this form.) While former employers may be afraid to say anything negative about a person, a glowing review can work well in the applicant's favor.

Background Checks

Beware that a former boss may be a good friend or even a relative. It has always been considered acceptable to exaggerate on résumés, but in recent years, some applicants have been found to be completely fabricating sections of their education and experience. Checking references is important.

To check an applicant's background, you can use an *authorization to release employment information*, *verification of education*, and *verification of licensure*. These forms are signed by the applicant, and grant you permission to obtain the information you need. The **AUTHORIZATION TO RELEASE EMPLOYMENT INFORMATION** can be used to check on employees for any type of job. (See the CD-ROM for a blank version of this form.) The **VERIFICATION OF EDUCATION** and **VERIFICATION OF LICENSURE** would only be necessary if the applicant's education or license was important to the job. (See the CD-ROM for blank versions of these forms.) However, you might check these things just to see if the employee was honest on the application.

To confirm an employee's legal status, you should use **FORM I-9**. (See the CD-ROM for a blank version of this form.) This shows you which documentation is adequate to check eligibility to work. If the applicant uses fake identification, you are not liable for hiring him or her, as long as you made an honest effort to be sure he or she produced the documentation required by law. This form should not be used until you have decided to hire a person.

Employer Identification Number

If you hire someone for more than a few hours work, you are required to register with the state and federal government to withhold taxes. Before you hire someone, you must obtain an employer identification number using **IRS FORM SS-4**. (See the CD-ROM for a blank version of this form.) Once you hire someone, you must have them complete IRS Form W-4 in order to calculate his or her withholding of income taxes.

Most states have their own registration and reporting requirements. Contact your state department of revenue for forms and applications.

Withholding, Social Security, and Medicare Taxes

If you need basic information on business tax returns, the IRS publishes a rather large booklet that answers most questions and is available free of charge. Call or write them and ask for Publication 334. If you have any questions, look up their toll-free number in the phone book under "United States Government/Internal Revenue Service." If you want more creative answers and tax-saving information, you should find a good local accountant. To get started, you will need to be familiar with the following:

- ◆ Employee's Withholding Allowance Certificate;
- ◆ federal tax deposit coupons;
- ◆ electronic filing;
- ◆ employer's quarterly tax return;
- ◆ wage and tax statement; and,
- ◆ earned income credit.

Employee's Withholding Allowance Certificate

You must have each employee fill out an *Employee's Withholding Allowance Certificate* (IRS Form W-4) to calculate the amount of federal taxes to be deducted and to obtain their Social Security numbers. (The number of allowances on this form is used with IRS Circular E, Publication 15, to figure out the exact deductions.)

Federal Tax Deposit Coupons

After taking withholdings from employees' wages, you must deposit them at a bank that is authorized to accept such funds. If at the end of any month you have over $1,000 in withheld taxes, including your contribution to FICA (Social Security and Medicare), you must make a deposit prior to the 15th of the following month. If on the 3rd, 7th, 11th, 15th, 19th, 22nd, or 25th of any month you have over $3,000 in withheld taxes, you must make a deposit within three banking days.

Electronic Filing

Each year, the IRS requires a few more forms to be filed electronically or over the telephone. When you receive your paper filing forms from the IRS, they will include your options for filing electronically or by telephone. In some cases, electronic filing may save time, but if your business is small and most of your numbers are zeros, it may be faster to mail in the paper forms.

Employer's Quarterly Tax Return

Each quarter, you must file Form 941, reporting your federal withholding and FICA taxes. If you owe more than $1,000 at the end of a quarter, you are required to make a deposit at the end of any month that you have $1,000 in withholding. The deposits are made to the Federal Reserve Bank or an authorized financial institution on Form 501. Most banks are authorized to accept deposits. If you owe more than $3,000 for any month, you must make a deposit at any point in the month in which you owe $3,000. After you file Form SS-4, the 941 forms will be sent to you automatically if you checked the box saying that you expect to have employees.

Wage and Tax Statement

At the end of each year, you are required to issue a W-2 Form to each employee. This form shows the amount of wages paid to the employee during the year, as well as the amounts withheld for taxes, Social Security, Medicare, and other purposes.

Earned Income Credit

Persons who are not liable to pay income tax may have the right to a check from the government because of the *earned income credit*. You are required to notify your employees of this. You can satisfy this requirement with one of the following:

- ◆ a W-2 Form with the notice on the back;
- ◆ a substitute for the W-2 Form with the notice on it;
- ◆ a copy of Notice 797; or,
- ◆ a written statement with the wording from Notice 797.

A Notice 797 can be downloaded from the IRS website at **www.irs.gov/pub/irs-pdf/n797.pdf.**

At the end of each year, you must file Form 940 or Form 940EZ. This is your annual report of federal unemployment taxes. You will receive an original form from the IRS.

Polygraph Tests

Under the federal *Employee Polygraph Protection Act,* you cannot require an employee or prospective employee to take a polygraph test unless you are in the armored car, guard, or pharmaceutical business.

Drug Tests

Under the Americans with Disabilities Act (ADA), drug testing can only be required of applicants who have been offered jobs conditioned upon passing the drug test.

New Hire Reporting

In order to track down parents who do not pay child support, a federal law was passed in 1996 that requires the reporting of new hires. The *Personal Responsibility and Work Opportunity Reconciliation Act of 1996* (PRWORA) provides that such information must be reported by employers to their state government.

Within twenty days of hiring a new employee, an employer must provide the state with information about the employee, including his or her name, Social Security number, and address. There is a special form that can be used for this reporting; however, an employer can simply use the Employee's Withholding Allowance Certificate (IRS Form W-4) for this purpose. Since this form must be filled out for all employees anyway, it would be pointless to use a separate form for the new hire reporting. The form changes every year, so contact the IRS (**www.irs.gov**) to get the latest version.

Employment Agreements

To avoid misunderstanding with employees, you should use an employment agreement or an employee handbook. These can spell out in detail the policies of your company and the rights of your employees. These agreements can protect your trade secrets and spell out clearly that employment can be terminated at any time by either party.

Make sure that your agreement is fair and clear, because you have the upper hand in this situation and you would not want a court to find that you abused that bargaining power with an unreasonable employee agreement.

If having an employee sign an agreement is awkward, you can usually obtain the same rights by putting the company policies in an employee manual. Each existing and new employee should be given a copy along with a letter stating that the rules apply to all employees, and that by accepting or continuing employment at your company, they agree to abide by the rules. Having an employee sign a receipt for the letter and manual is proof that he or she received it.

One danger of an employment agreement or handbook is that it may be interpreted to create a long-term employment contract. To avoid this, be sure that you clearly state in the agreement or handbook that the employment is *at will* and can be terminated at any time by either party.

Some other things to consider in an employment agreement or handbook are:
   ◆ what the salary and other compensation will be;
   ◆ what the hours of employment will be;
   ◆ what the probationary period will be;
   ◆ that the employee cannot sign any contracts binding the employer; and,
   ◆ that the employee agrees to arbitration rather than filing a lawsuit if serious disagreements arise.

Firing

In most cases, unless you have a contract with an employee for a set time period, you can fire him or her at any time. This is only fair, since the employee can quit at any time. This type of employment is called *at will*. You should make it clear when offering a job to someone that, upon acceptance, he or she will be an at-will employee. The exceptions to this are if you fired someone based on illegal discrimination, for filing some sort of health or safety complaint, or for refusing your or another supervisor's sexual advances.

Independent Contractors

One way to avoid problems with employees and taxes at the same time is to have all of your work done through independent contractors. This can relieve you of most of the burdens of employment laws, as well as the obligation to pay Social Security and Medicare taxes for the workers.

An independent contractor is, in effect, a separate business that you pay to do a job. You pay them just as you pay any company from which you buy products or services. At the end of the year, if the amount paid exceeds $600, you must issue a 1099 form, which is similar to the W-2 that you would issue to employees.

This may seem too good to be true, and in some situations it is. The IRS does not like independent contractor arrangements, because it is too easy for the independent contractors to cheat on their taxes. To limit the use of independent contractors, the IRS has strict regulations on who may and may not be classified as an independent contractor. Also, companies who do not appear to pay enough in wages for their field of business are audited.

Using independent contractors for jobs not traditionally done by independent contractors puts you at high risk for an IRS audit. For example, you could not get away with hiring a secretary as an independent contractor. One of the most important factors considered in determining if a worker can be an independent contractor is the amount of control the company has over his or her work. If you need someone to paint your building and you agree to pay a certain price to have it done according to the painter's own methods and schedule, you can pay the painter as an independent contractor. However, if you tell the painter when and how to do the work, and provide the tools and materials, the painter will be classified as an employee.

If you just need some typing done and you take it to a typing service and pick it up when it is ready, you will be safe in treating those workers as independent contractors. However, if you need someone to come into your office to type on your machine at your schedule, you will probably be required to treat that person as an employee for tax purposes.

The IRS has a form you can use in determining if a person is an employee or an independent contractor, called DETERMINATION OF WORKER STATUS FOR PURPOSES OF FEDERAL EMPLOYMENT TAXES AND INCOME TAX WITHHOLDING (IRS FORM SS-8). (See the CD-ROM for a blank version of this form, and check **www.irs.gov** for the most recent version.)

Independent Contractors vs. Employees

In deciding whether to make use of independent contractors or employees, you should weigh the following advantages and disadvantages.

Advantages.
- *Lower taxes.* You do not have to pay Social Security, Medicare, unemployment, or other employee taxes.
- *Less paperwork.* You do not have to handle federal withholding deposits or the monthly employer returns to the state or federal government.
- *Less insurance.* You do not have to pay workers' compensation insurance or insurance against their possible liabilities.
- *More flexibility.* You can use independent contractors only when you need them.

Disadvantages.
- *Scrutiny from the IRS.* The IRS and state tax offices are strict about which workers can be qualified as independent contractors. They will audit companies whose use of independent contractors does not appear to be legitimate.

◆ *Penalties for improper use.* If your use of independent contractors is found to be improper, you may have to pay back taxes and penalties, and may have problems with your pension plan.

◆ *Potential for injury lawsuits.* While employees usually cannot sue you for their injuries (if you have covered them with workers' compensation), independent contractors can sue you if their injuries were your fault.

◆ *Fewer creative works rights.* If you are paying someone to produce a creative work (writing, photography, artwork), you receive fewer rights to the work of an independent contractor.

◆ *Less control.* You have less control over the work of an independent contractor and less flexibility in terminating him or her if you are not satisfied that the job is being done the way you require.

◆ *Less loyalty.* You have less loyalty from an independent contractor—who works sporadically for you and possibly others—than you have from your own full-time employees.

For some businesses, the advantages outweigh the disadvantages. For others, they do not. Consider your business plans and the consequences from each type of arrangement. Keep in mind that it will be easier to start with independent contractors and switch to employees than to hire employees and have to fire them to hire independent contractors.

Temporary Workers

Another way to avoid the hassles of hiring employees is to get workers from a temporary agency. In this arrangement, you may pay a higher amount per hour for the work, but the agency will take care of all of the tax and insurance requirements. Since these can be expensive and time-consuming, the extra cost may be well worth it.

Whether or not temporary workers will work for you depends upon the type of business you are in and tasks you need performed. For such jobs as sales management, you would probably want someone who will stay with you long-term and develop relationships with the buyers, but for order fulfillment, temporary workers might work out well.

Another advantage of temporary workers is that you can easily stop using those who do not work out well for you. Conversely, if you find one who is ideal, you may be able to hire him or her on a full-time basis.

In recent years, a new wrinkle has developed in the temporary worker area. Many large companies are beginning to use them because they are so much cheaper than paying the benefits demanded by full-time employees. For example, Microsoft Corp. had as many as 6,000 temporary workers, some of whom worked for them for years. Some of the temporary workers won a lawsuit that declared they are really employees and are entitled to the same benefits of other employees (such as pension plans).

The law is not yet settled in this area, regarding what arrangements will result in a temporary worker being declared an employee. That will take several more court cases, some of which have already been filed. A few things you can do to protect yourself include the following.

- ◆ Be sure that any of your benefit plans make it clear that they do not apply to workers obtained through temporary agencies.
- ◆ Do not keep the same temporary workers for longer than a year.
- ◆ Do not list temporary workers in any employee directories or hold them out to the public as your employees.
- ◆ Do not allow them to use your business cards or stationery.

Discrimination Laws

There are numerous federal laws forbidding discrimination based upon race, sex, pregnancy, color, religion, national origin, age, or disability. The laws apply to both hiring and firing, and to employment practices such as salaries, promotions, and benefits. Most of these laws only apply to an employer who has fifteen or more employees for twenty weeks of a calendar year, or has federal contracts or subcontracts. Therefore, you most likely will not be required to comply with the law immediately upon opening your business. However, there are similar state laws that may apply to your business that have a lower employee threshold.

One exception to the fifteen or more employees rule is the *Equal Pay Act*. This act applies to employers with two or more employees, and requires that women be paid the same as men in the same type of job.

Employers with fifteen or more employees are required to display a poster regarding discrimination. This poster is available from the Equal Employment Opportunity Commission on their website at **www.dol.gov/esa/regs/compliance/posters/ eeo.htm**. Employers with one hundred or more employees are required to file an annual report with the EEOC.

Discriminatory Interview Questions

When hiring employees, some questions are illegal or inadvisable to ask. The following data *should not* be collected on your employment application or in your interviews, unless the information is somehow directly tied to the duties of the job.

- ◆ Do not ask about an applicant's citizenship or place of birth. However, after hiring an employee, you must ask about his or her right to work in this country.
- ◆ Do not ask a female applicant her maiden name. You can ask if she has been known by any other name in order to do a background check.
- ◆ Do not ask if applicants have children, plan to have them, or have child care. You can ask if an applicant will be able to work the required hours.
- ◆ Do not ask if the applicant has religious objections for working Saturday or Sunday. You can mention if the job requires such hours and ask whether the applicant can meet this job requirement.
- ◆ Do not ask an applicant's age. You can ask if an applicant is age 18 or over, or if it is a liquor-related job, you can ask if the applicant is age 21 or over.
- ◆ Do not ask an applicant's weight.
- ◆ Do not ask if an applicant has AIDS or is HIV-positive.
- ◆ Do not ask if the applicant has filed a workers' compensation claim.
- ◆ Do not ask about the applicant's previous health problems.
- ◆ Do not ask if the applicant is married or whether the spouse would object to the job, hours, or duties.

◆ Do not ask if the applicant owns a home, furniture, or car, as it is considered racially discriminatory.

◆ Do not ask if the applicant was ever arrested. You can ask if the applicant was ever convicted of a crime.

ADA

Under the *Americans with Disabilities Act of 1990* (ADA), employers who do not make *reasonable accommodations* for disabled employees will face fines of up to $100,000, as well as other civil penalties and civil damage awards.

While the goal of creating more opportunities for the disabled is a good one, the result has put all of the costs of achieving this goal on businesses that are faced with disabled applicants. In fact, studies done since the law was passed have shown that employers have hired fewer disabled applicants than before the law was passed, possibly due to the costs of reasonable accommodations and the fear of being taken to court.

The ADA is very vague. When it passed, some feared it could be taken to ridiculous lengths—such as forcing companies to hire blind applicants for jobs that require reading, and then forcing them to hire people to read for the blind employees. In the years since its enactment, some of the critics' fears have been met. In some famous rulings, the EEOC said:

◆ rude, disruptive, and chronically late employees could be protected by the ADA if they had some type of mental disability;

◆ recovering drug addicts and alcoholics are protected by the ADA;

◆ obesity can be a disability covered by the ADA;

◆ workers who are disturbed by the sight of other workers because of emotional imbalance must be given private work areas; and,

◆ airlines cannot discriminate against persons blind in one eye when hiring pilots.

When the ADA was passed, it was estimated that 3 million Americans were blind, deaf, or in wheelchairs, but it has been estimated that the ADA now applies to 49 million Americans with every type of physical or mental impairment. Of the

ADA cases that go to court, 92% are won by businesses. While this may sound good, considering the cost of going to court, the expense of this litigation is devastating for the businesses. Many of these lawsuits occur because the law is worded so vaguely.

The ADA currently applies to employers with fifteen or more employees. Employers who need more than fifteen employees might want to consider contracting with independent contractors to avoid problems with this law, particularly if the number of employees is only slightly larger than fifteen.

For more information on how this law affects your business, see the U.S. Department of Justice website at **www.usdoj.gov/crt/ada/business.htm**.

Tax Benefits

There are three types of tax credits to help small businesses with the burden of these laws.

- ◆ Businesses can deduct up to $15,000 a year for making their premises accessible to the disabled and can depreciate the rest. (Internal Revenue Code (I.R.C.) Section 190.)
- ◆ Small businesses (under $1,000,000 in revenue and under thirty employees) can get a tax credit each year for 50% of the cost of making their premises accessible to the disabled, but this only applies to the amount between $250 and $10,500.
- ◆ Small businesses can get a credit of up to 40% of the first $6,000 of wages paid to certain new employees who qualify through the Pre-Screening Notice and Certification Request (IRS Form 8850).

Records

To protect against potential claims of discrimination, all employers should keep detailed records showing reasons for hiring or not hiring applicants, and for firing employees.

Sexual Harassment

As an employer you can be liable for the acts of your employees. One of the latest types of acts that employers have been help liable for is sexual harassment of customers, employees, and others. While you cannot control every act of every employee, if you indicate to employees that such behavior is unacceptable and set up a system to resolve complaints, you will do much to protect yourself against lawsuits.

The EEOC has held the following in sexual harassment cases.

◆ The victim as well as the harasser may be a woman or a man.

◆ The victim does not have to be of the opposite sex.

◆ The harasser can be the victim's supervisor, an agent of the employer, a supervisor in another area, a coworker, or a nonemployee.

◆ The victim does not have to be the person harassed, but could be anyone affected by the offensive conduct.

◆ Unlawful sexual harassment may occur without economic injury to or discharge of the victim.

◆ The harasser's conduct must be unwelcome.

Some of the actions that have been considered harassment are:

◆ displaying sexually explicit posters in the workplace;

◆ requiring female employees to wear revealing uniforms;

◆ rating the sexual attractiveness of female employees as they pass male employees' desks;

◆ continued sexual jokes and innuendos;

◆ demands for sexual favors from subordinates;

◆ unwelcomed sexual propositions or flirtation;

◆ unwelcomed physical contact; and,

◆ whistling or leering at members of the opposite sex.

In 1993, the United States Supreme Court ruled that an employee can make a claim for sexual harassment even without proof of a specific injury. However, lower federal courts in more recent cases have dismissed cases where no specific injury was shown. These new cases may indicate that the pendulum has stopped moving toward expanded rights for the employee.

On the other hand, another recent case ruled that an employer can be liable for the harassment of an employee by a supervisor—even if the employer was unaware of the supervisor's conduct—if the employer did not have a system in place to allow complaints against harassment. This area of law is still developing, but to avoid a possible lawsuit, you should be aware of the things that could potentially cause liability and avoid them.

Some things a business can do to protect against claims of sexual harassment include the following.

- Distribute a written policy against all kinds of sexual harassment to all employees.
- Encourage employees to report all incidents of sexual harassment.
- Ensure there is no retaliation against those who complain.
- Make clear that your policy is *zero tolerance.*
- Explain that sexual harassment includes both requests for sexual favors and a work environment that some employees may consider hostile.
- Allow employees to report harassment to someone other than their immediate supervisor, in case that person is involved in the harassment.
- Promise as much confidentiality as possible to complainants.

Wage and Hour Laws

The *Fair Labor Standards Act* (FLSA) applies to all employers who are engaged in *interstate commerce* or in the production of goods for interstate commerce (anything that will cross the state line), and all employees of hospitals, schools, residential facilities for the disabled or aged, and public agencies. It also applies to all employees of enterprises that gross $500,000 or more per year.

While many small businesses might not think they are engaged in interstate commerce, the laws have been interpreted so broadly that nearly any use of the mails, interstate telephone service, or other interstate services, however minor, is enough to bring a business under the law.

Minimum Wage

The federal wage and hour laws are contained in the federal *Fair Labor Standards Act*. In 1996, Congress passed and President Clinton signed legislation raising the minimum wage to $5.15 an hour beginning September 1, 1997. At the time this was written, Congress had voted to raise the minimum wage to $7.25 an hour, but it had yet been signed into law. Several states also have their own minimum wage laws. Most match whatever the federal government amount is, but some states require a higher minimum wage. Check with your state's laws to verify the amount you must pay and to see if any exemption or lower amounts (like employees earning tips) may apply to you.

Exempt Employees

While nearly all businesses are covered, certain employees are exempt from the FLSA. Exempt employees include those who are considered executives, administrators, managers, professionals, computer professionals, and outside salespeople.

Whether or not one of these exceptions applies to a particular employee is a complicated legal question. Thousands of court cases have been decided on this issue, but they have given no clear answers. In one case, a person could be determined to be exempt because of his or her duties, but in another, a person with the same duties could be found not exempt.

One thing that is clear is that the determination is made on the employee's function, and not just the job title. You cannot make a secretary exempt by calling him or her a manager, if most of his or her duties are clerical. For more information, see the Department of Labor website **www.dol.gov/esa/whd/flsa**.

On the Internet you can obtain information on the Department of Labor's *Employment Law Guide* at **www.dol.gov/asp/programs/guide/main.htm**.

Overtime

The general rule is that employees who work more than forty hours a week must be paid time-and-a-half for hours worked over forty. However, there are many exemptions to this general rule based on salary and position. These exceptions were completely revised in 2004, and an explanation of the changes, including a tutorial video, are available at **www.dol.gov/esa**. For answers to questions about the law, call the Department of Labor at 866-4-USA-DOL (866-487-2365).

Pension and Benefit Laws

There are no laws requiring small businesses to provide any type of special benefits to employees. Such benefits are given to attract and keep good employees. With pension plans, the main concern is if you do start one, it must comply with federal tax laws.

There are no federal laws that require employees be given holidays off. You can require them to work Thanksgiving and Christmas, and can dock their pay or fire them for failing to show up. Of course, you will not have much luck keeping employees with such a policy.

Holidays

Most companies give full-time employees a certain number of paid holidays, such as: New Year's Day (January 1); Memorial Day (last Monday in May); Fourth of July; Labor Day (first Monday in September); Thanksgiving (fourth Thursday in November); and Christmas (December 25). Some employers include other holidays, such as Martin Luther King Jr.'s birthday (January 15); President's Day; and, Columbus Day. If one of the holidays falls on a Saturday or Sunday, many employers give the preceding Friday or following Monday off. You need to decide what holidays you want to give your employees.

Sick Days

There is no federal law mandating that an employee be paid for time that he or she is home sick. The situation seems to be that the larger the company, the more paid sick leave is allowed. Part-time workers rarely get sick leave, and small business sick leave is usually limited for the simple reason that they cannot afford to pay for time that employees do not work.

Some small companies have an official policy of no paid sick leave, but when an important employee misses a day because he or she is clearly sick, it is paid.

Breaks

There are no federal laws requiring coffee breaks or lunch breaks. However, it is common sense that employees will be more productive if they have reasonable breaks for nourishment or to use the toilet facilities.

Pension Plans and Retirement Accounts

Few new small businesses can afford to provide pension plans for their employees. The first concern of a small business is usually how the owner can shelter income in a pension plan for him or herself without having to set up a pension plan for an employee. Under most pension plans, this is not allowed. The following are some of the most common retirement accounts.

IRA. Any individual can put up to $4,000 ($5,000 if age 50 or over) in an Individual Retirement Account (IRA). Unless the person, or his or her spouse, is covered by a company pension plan and has income over a certain amount, the amount put into the account is fully tax deductible.

Roth IRA. Contributions to a Roth IRA are not tax deductible, but when the money is taken out, it is not taxable. People who expect to still have taxable income when they withdraw from their IRA can benefit from these.

SEP IRA, SAR-SEP IRA, SIMPLE IRA. With these types of retirement accounts, a person can put a much greater amount into a retirement plan and deduct it from their taxable income. Employees must also be covered by such plans, but certain employees are exempt, so it is sometimes possible to use these for the owners alone. The best source for more information is a mutual fund company (such as Vanguard, Fidelity, or Dreyfus) or a local bank, which can set up the plan and provide you with all of the rules. These have an advantage over qualified plans (discussed below) since they do not have the high annual fees.

Qualified retirement plans. Qualified retirement plans are 401(k) plans, Keogh plans, and corporate retirement plans. These are covered by the *Employee Retirement Income Security Act* (ERISA), which is a complicated law meant to protect employee pension plans. Congress did not want employees who contributed to pension plans all their lives ending up with nothing if the plan went bankrupt. The law is so complicated and the penalties so severe that some companies are cancelling their pension plans, and applications for new plans are a fraction of what they were previously. However, many banks and mutual funds have created *canned plans*, which can be used instead of drafting one from scratch. Still, the fees for administering them are steep. Check with a bank or mutual fund for details.

Family and Medical Leave Law

To assist business owners in deciding what type of leave to offer their employees, Congress passed the *Family and Medical Leave Act of 1993* (FMLA). This law requires an employee to be given up to twelve weeks of unpaid leave when:

- ◆ the employee or employee's spouse has a child;
- ◆ the employee adopts a child or takes in a foster child;
- ◆ the employee needs to care for an ill spouse, child, or parent; or,
- ◆ the employee becomes seriously ill.

The law only applies to employers with fifty or more employees. Also, the top 10% of an employer's salaried employees can be denied this leave because of the disruption in business their loss could cause.

Child Labor Laws

The federal Fair Labor Standards Act also contains rules regarding the hiring of children. The basic rules are that children under 16 years old may not be hired at all except in a few jobs, such as acting and newspaper delivery, and those under 18 may not be hired for dangerous jobs. Children may not work more than three hours a day or eighteen hours a week in a school week, or more than eight hours a day or forty hours a week in a non-school week. If you plan to hire children, you should check the Fair Labor Standards Act, which is in United States Code (U.S.C.), Title 29, and the related regulations, which are in the Code of Federal Regulations (C.F.R.), Title 29.

Immigration Laws

There are strict penalties for any business that hires aliens who are not eligible to work. You must verify both the identity and the employment eligibility of anyone you hire by using the EMPLOYMENT ELIGIBILITY VERIFICATION (FORM I-9). (See the CD-ROM for a blank version of this form.) Both you and the employee must fill out the form, and you must check an employee's identification cards or papers. Fines for hiring illegal aliens range from $250 to $2,000 for the first offense and up to $10,000 for the third offense. Failure to maintain the proper paperwork may result in a fine of up to $1,000. The law does not apply to independent contractors with whom you may contract, and it does not penalize you if the employee used fake identification.

There are also penalties that apply to employers of four or more persons for discriminating against eligible applicants because they appear foreign or because of their national origin or citizenship status.

For more information, call 800-357-2099. For the *Handbook for Employers and Instructions for Completing Form I-9,* check the *United States Citizenship and Immigration Services* (USCIS) website at **www.uscis.gov**.

Foreign Employees

If you wish to hire employees who are foreign citizens and are not able to provide the proper documentation, they must first obtain a work visa from USCIS.

Work visas for foreigners are not easy to get. Millions of people around the globe would like to come to the U.S. to work, but the laws are designed to keep most of them out to protect the jobs of American citizens.

Whether or not a person can get a work visa depends on whether there is a shortage of U.S. workers available to fill the job. For jobs requiring few or no skills, it is practically impossible to get a visa. For highly skilled jobs, such as nurses and physical therapists, and for those of exceptional ability, such as Nobel Prize winners and Olympic medalists, obtaining a visa is fairly easy.

There are several types of visas, and different rules for different countries. For example, NAFTA has made it easier for some types of workers to enter the U.S. from Canada and Mexico. For some positions, the shortage of workers is assumed by the USCIS. For others, a business must first advertise a position available in the United States. Only after no qualified persons apply can it hire someone from another country.

The visa system is complicated and subject to regular change. If you wish to hire a foreign worker, you should consult with an immigration specialist or a book on the subject.

Hiring Off the Books

Because of the taxes, insurance, and red tape involved with hiring employees, some new businesses hire people *off the books*. They pay them in cash and never admit they are employees. While the cash paid in wages would not be deductible, they consider this a smaller cost than compliance. Some even use off the books receipts to cover it.

Except when your spouse or child is giving you some temporary help, this is a terrible idea. Hiring people off the books can result in civil fines, loss of insurance coverage, and even criminal penalties. When engaged in dangerous work, like roofing or using power tools, you are risking millions of dollars in potential liability if a worker is killed or seriously injured. It may be more costly and time-consuming to comply with the employment laws, but if you are concerned with long-term growth with less risk, it is the wiser way to go.

Federal Contracts

Companies that do work for the federal government are subject to several laws.

The *Davis-Bacon Act* requires contractors engaged in U.S. government construction projects to pay wages and benefits that are equal to or better than the prevailing wages in the area.

The *McNamara-O'Hara Service Contract Act* sets wages and other labor standards for contractors furnishing services to agencies of the U.S. government.

The *Walsh-Healey Public Contracts Act* requires the Department of Labor to settle disputes regarding manufacturers supplying products to the U.S. government.

Miscellaneous Laws

In addition to the broad categories of laws affecting businesses, there are several other federal laws that you should be familiar with that regulate affirmative action, layoffs, unions, and informational posters.

Affirmative Action

In most cases, the federal government does not tell employers who they must hire. The only situation in which a small business would need to comply with affirmative action requirements would be if it accepted federal contracts or subcontracts. These requirements could include hiring minorities or veterans of the conflict in Vietnam.

Layoffs

Companies with one hundred or more full-time employees at one location are subject to the *Worker Adjustment and Retraining Notification Act*. This law requires a sixty-day notification prior to certain layoffs and has other strict provisions.

Unions

The *National Labor Relations Act of 1935* gives employees the right to organize a union or to join one. (29 U.S.C. Secs. 151 et seq.) There are things employers can do to protect themselves, but you should consult a labor attorney or a book on the subject before taking action that might be illegal and result in fines.

Poster Laws

Poster laws require certain posters to be displayed to inform employees of their rights. Not all businesses are required to display all posters, but the following list should be of help.

- ◆ All employers must display the wage and hour poster available from the U.S. Department of Labor at **www.dol.gov/esa**.
- ◆ Employers with fifteen or more employees for twenty weeks of the year must display the sex, race, religion, and ethnic discrimination poster, as well as the age discrimination poster, available from the EEOC at **www.eeoc.gov/publications.html**.
- ◆ Employers with federal contracts or subcontracts of $10,000 or more must display the sex, race, religion, and ethnic discrimination poster, plus a poster regarding Vietnam Era Veterans (available from the local federal contracting office).
- ◆ Employers with government contracts subject to the *Service Contract Act* or the *Public Contracts Act* must display a notice to employees working on government contracts available from the Employment Standards Division at **www.dol.gov/esa/whd**.

State Law

Be sure to check with your state governmental offices and websites for information on state employment and labor laws that may apply to your business.

Chapter 13:

Advertising and Promotion Laws

Because of the unscrupulous and deceptive advertising techniques of some companies, as well as the multitude of con artists trying to steal from innocent consumers, numerous federal and state statutes have been enacted that make it unlawful to use improper advertising and promotional techniques in soliciting business.

Advertising Laws and Rules

The federal government regulates advertising through the *Federal Trade Commission* (FTC). The rules are contained in the *Code of Federal Regulations* (C.F.R.). You can find these rules in most law libraries and many public libraries. If you plan on doing any advertising that you think may be questionable, you might want to check the rules. As you read the rules, you will probably think of many violations you see every day.

Federal rules do not apply to every business, and small businesses that operate only within the state and do not use the postal service may be exempt. However, many of the federal rules have been adopted into law by various states. Therefore, a violation could be prosecuted by the state rather than the federal government.

Some of the important rules are summarized in this section. If you wish to learn more details about the rules and whether your state has passed similar laws, you should obtain copies from your library.

Deceptive Pricing

When prices are being compared, it is required that actual and not inflated prices are used. For example, if an object would usually be sold for $7, you should not first offer it for $10 and then start offering it at 30% off. It is considered misleading to suggest that a discount from list price is a bargain if the item is seldom actually sold at list price. If most surrounding stores sell an item for $7, it is considered misleading to say it has a retail value of $10, even if there are some stores elsewhere selling it at that price. (C.F.R., Title 16, Ch. I, Part 233.)

Bait Advertising

Bait advertising is placing an ad when you do not really want the respondents to buy the product offered, but want them to switch to another item. (C.F.R., Title 16, Ch. I, Part 238.)

Use of "Free," "Half-Off," and Similar Words

Use of words such as "free," "1¢ sale," "half-off," and the like must not be misleading. This means that the regular price must not include a mark-up to cover the free item. The seller must expect to sell the product without the free item at some time in the future. (C.F.R., Title 16, Ch. I, Part 251.)

Substantiation of Claims

The FTC requires that advertisers be able to substantiate their claims. Some information on this policy is contained on the Internet at **www.ftc.gov/bcp/guides/ ad3subst.htm**. (C.F.R., Title 16; Federal Regulations (F.R.), Title 48, Page 10471 (1983).)

Endorsements

This rule forbids endorsements that are misleading. An example is a quote from a film review that is used in such a way as to change the substance of the review. It is not necessary to use the exact words of the person endorsing the product, as long as the opinion is not distorted. If a product is changed, an endorsement that does not apply to the new version cannot be used. For some items, such as drugs, claims cannot be used without scientific proof. Endorsements by organizations cannot be used unless one is sure that the membership holds the same opinion. (C.F.R., Title 16, Ch. I, Part 255.)

Unfairness

Any advertising practices that can be deemed to be *unfair* are forbidden by the FTC. An explanation of this policy is located on the Internet at **www.ftc.gov/bcp/policystmt/ad-unfair.htm**. (15 U.S.C. Section 45.)

Negative Option Plans

When a seller uses a sales system in which the buyer must notify the seller if he or she does not want the goods, the seller must provide the buyer with a form to decline the sale and at least ten days in which to decline. Bonus merchandise must be shipped promptly, and the seller must promptly terminate shipment for any who so requests after completion of the contract. (C.F.R., Title 16, Ch. I, Part 425.)

Laser Eye Surgery

Under the laws governing deceptive advertising, the FTC and the FDA are regulating the advertising of laser eye surgery. Anyone involved in this area should obtain a copy of these rules. They are located on the Internet at **www.ftc.gov/bcp/guides/eyecare2.htm**. (15 U.S.C. Sections 45, 52–57.)

Food and Dietary Supplements

Under the *Nutritional Labeling Education Act of 1990*, the FTC and the FDA regulate the packaging and advertising of food and dietary products. Anyone involved in this area should obtain a copy of these rules. They are located on the Internet at **www.ftc.gov/bcp/menu-health.htm**. (21 U.S.C. Section 343.)

Jewelry and Precious Metals

The FTC has numerous rules governing the sale and advertising of jewelry and precious metals. Anyone in this business should obtain a copy of these rules. They are located on the Internet at **www.ftc.gov/bcp/guides/jewel-gd.htm**. (F.R., Title 61, Page 27212.)

Internet Sales Laws

There are not yet specific laws governing Internet transactions that are different from laws governing other transactions. The FTC feels that its current rules regarding deceptive advertising, substantiation, disclaimers, refunds, and related matters must be followed by Internet businesses, and that consumers are adequately protected by them. For some specific guidelines on Internet advertising, see the FTC's site at **www.ftc.gov/bcp/conline/pubs/buspubs/ruleroad.htm**.

Email Advertising

The *Controlling the Assault of Non-Solicited Pornography And Marketing Act of 2003* (CAN-SPAM) has put numerous controls on how you can use email to solicit business for your company. It requires unsolicited commercial email messages to be labeled, and the message must include opt-out instructions and the sender's physical address. Some of the prohibited activities under the Act are:

- ◆ false or misleading information in an email;
- ◆ deceptive subject heading;
- ◆ failure to include a functioning return address;
- ◆ mailing to someone who has asked not to receive solicitations;
- ◆ failure to include a valid postal address;
- ◆ omitting an opt-out procedure;
- ◆ failure to clearly mark the email as advertising; and,
- ◆ including sexual material without adequate warnings.

Some of the provisions contain criminal penalties as well as civil fines.

For more information on the CAN-SPAM Act, see **www.ftc.gov/bcp/conline/ pubs/buspubs/canspam.htm**. For text of the Act plus other spam laws around the world, see **www.spamlaws.com**. Also see Chapter 10 for more information on Internet advertising.

Home Solicitation Laws

The Federal Trade Commission has rules governing door-to-door sales. In any such sale, it is a deceptive trade practice to fail to furnish a receipt explaining the sale (in the language of the presentation), as is failure to give notice that there is a right to back out of the contract within three days, known as a *right of rescission*. The notice must be supplied in duplicate, must be in at least 10-point type, and must be captioned either "Notice of Right to Cancel" or "Notice of Cancellation." The notice must be worded as the example on page 117 illustrates.

NOTICE OF CANCELLATION

_____
Date

YOU MAY CANCEL THIS TRANSACTION, WITHOUT ANY PENALTY OR OBLIGA-TION, WITHIN THREE BUSINESS DAYS FROM THE ABOVE DATE.

IF YOU CANCEL, ANY PROPERTY TRADED IN, ANY PAYMENTS MADE BY YOU UNDER THE CONTRACT OR SALE, AND ANY NEGOTIABLE INSTRUMENT EXECUTED BY YOU WILL BE RETURNED TO YOU WITHIN 10 BUSINESS DAYS FOLLOWING RECEIPT BY THE SELLER OF YOUR CANCELLATION NOTICE, AND ANY SECURITY INTEREST ARISING OUT OF THE TRANSACTION WILL BE CANCELLED.

IF YOU CANCEL, YOU MUST MAKE AVAILABLE TO THE SELLER AT YOUR RESI-DENCE, IN SUBSTANTIALLY AS GOOD CONDITION AS WHEN RECEIVED, ANY GOODS DELIVERED TO YOU UNDER THIS CONTRACT OR SALE; OR YOU MAY, IF YOU WISH, COMPLY WITH THE INSTRUCTIONS OF THE SELLER REGARDING THE RETURN SHIPMENT OF THE GOODS AT THE SELLER'S EXPENSE AND RISK.

IF YOU DO MAKE THE GOODS AVAILABLE TO THE SELLER AND THE SELLER DOES NOT PICK THEM UP WITHIN 20 DAYS OF THE DATE OF YOUR NOTICE OF CANCELLATION, YOU MAY RETAIN OR DISPOSE OF THE GOODS WITHOUT ANY FURTHER OBLIGATION. IF YOU FAIL TO MAKE THE GOODS AVAILABLE TO THE SELLER, OR IF YOU AGREE TO RETURN THE GOODS AND FAIL TO DO SO, THEN YOU REMAIN LIABLE FOR PERFORMANCE OF ALL OBLIGATIONS UNDER THE CONTRACT.

TO CANCEL THIS TRANSACTION, MAIL OR DELIVER A SIGNED AND DATED COPY OF THIS CANCELLATION NOTICE OR ANY OTHER WRITTEN NOTICE, OR SEND A TELEGRAM, TO _____(name of seller), AT _____(address of seller's place of business) NOT LATER THAN MIDNIGHT OF _____ (date).

I HEREBY CANCEL THIS TRANSACTION.

_____　　_____
(Buyer's signature)　　　　　　　　　　　　　　　(Date)

The seller must complete the notice and orally inform the buyer of the right to cancel. He or she cannot misrepresent the right to cancel, assign the contract until the fifth business day, or include a confession of judgment in the contract. For more specific details, see the rules contained in the Code of Federal Regulations, Title 16, Chapter I, Part 429.

Telephone Solicitation Laws

Telephone solicitations are governed by the *Telephone Consumer Protection Act* (47 U.S.C. Sec. 227) and the Federal Communications Commission rules implementing the Act (C.F.R., Title 47, Sec. 64.1200). Violators of the act can be sued for $500 damages by consumers and can be fined $10,000 by the FCC. Some of the requirements under the law include the following.

- ◆ Calls can only be made between 8 a.m. and 9 p.m.
- ◆ Solicitors must keep a *do not call* list and honor requests not to call.
- ◆ There must be a written policy that the parties called are told the name of the caller, the caller's business name and phone number or address, that the call is a sales call, and the nature of the goods or services.
- ◆ Personnel must be trained in the policies.
- ◆ Recorded messages cannot be used to call residences.

In 2003, the FCC introduced the national *Do Not Call Registry*, in which individuals could register their telephone numbers and prohibit certain telephone solicitors from calling the registered numbers. Once a person registers a telephone number, it remains on the registry for five years. Telemarketing firms can receive heavy fines for violating the registry statute, with fines ranging up to $11,000 per violation. Not all telephone solicitations are barred, however. The following solicitors may still contact a person whose telephone number has been entered in the registry:

- ◆ calls from companies with which the registered person has a prior business relationship;
- ◆ calls for which the recipient has given written consent;
- ◆ calls that do not include advertisements; and,
- ◆ calls from charitable organizations.

It is illegal under the Act to send advertising faxes to anyone who has not consented to receiving such faxes or is not an existing customer.

Weights and Labeling

All food products are required to have labels displaying information on the product's nutritional values, such as calories, fat, and protein. For most products, the label must be in the required format so that consumers can easily compare products. However, if such a format will not fit on the product label, the information may be in another format that is easily readable.

Federal rules require metric measurement be included on products. Under these rules, metric measures do not have to be the first measurement on the container, but they must be included. Food items that are packaged as they are sold (such as delicatessen items) do not have to contain metric labels.

Chapter 14:

Payment and Collection

Depending on the business you are in, you may be paid by cash, checks, credit cards, or some sort of financing arrangement, such as a promissory note or mortgage. Both state and federal laws affect the type of payments you collect, and failure to follow the laws can cost you considerably.

Cash

Cash is probably the easiest form of payment and it is subject to few restrictions. The most important one is that you keep an accurate accounting of your cash transactions and that you report all of your cash income on your tax return. Recent efforts to stop the drug trade have resulted in some serious penalties for failing to report cash transactions and for money laundering. The laws are so sweeping that even if you deal in cash in an ordinary business, you may violate the law and face huge fines and imprisonment.

The most important law to be concerned with is the one requiring the filing of the Report of Cash Payments over $10,000 (IRS Form 8300). (A copy of form 8300 can be found at **www.irs.gov**.) If one person pays you with $10,000 or more in cash, you are required to file this form. A transaction does not have to happen in one day. If a person brings you smaller amounts of cash that add up to $10,000 and the government can construe them as one transaction, then the form must be filed. Under this law, *cash* also includes travelers' checks and money orders, but not cashiers' checks or bank checks.

Credit Cards

In our buy now, pay later society, charge cards can add greatly to your sales potential, especially with large, discretionary purchases. For MasterCard, Visa, and Discover, the fees businesses must pay to accept these cards are about 2%, and this amount is easily paid for by the extra purchases that the cards allow. American Express charges 4% to 5%. (You may decide this is not worth paying, since almost everyone who has an American Express card also has another card.)

For businesses that have a retail outlet, there is usually no problem getting merchant status. Most commercial banks can handle it. Discover can also set you up to accept their card as well as MasterCard and Visa, and they will wire the money into your bank account daily.

For mail order businesses, especially those operating out of the home, it is much harder to get merchant status because of the number of scams in which large amounts are charged, no products are shipped, and the company folds. Today, things are a little better. Some companies are even soliciting merchants. However, beware of those that charge exorbitant fees (such as $5 or $10 per order for "processing"). American Express will accept mail order companies operating out of the home. However, not as many people have their cards as others.

Some companies open a small storefront (or share one) to get merchant status, then process mostly mail orders. The processors usually do not want to accept you if you will do more than 50% mail order business; but if you do not have many complaints, you may be allowed to process mostly mail orders. Whatever you do, keep your charge customers happy so that they do not complain.

You might be tempted to try to run your charges through another business. This may be all right if you actually sell your products through the other businesses, but if you run your business charges through that account, the other business may lose its merchant status. People who bought a book by mail from you and then find a charge on their statement from a florist shop will probably call the credit card company saying that they never bought anything from the florist shop. If you have too many of these, the account will be closed.

A new money-making scheme by the credit card companies is to offer business credit cards that the merchants are charged a higher fee for accepting. To make these more profitable, the credit card companies are telling customers they are not allowed to use their personal credit cards for business purposes. To keep your processing fees down, you can tell your customers you prefer personal, not business, credit cards.

Financing Laws

Some businesses can more easily make sales if they finance the purchases themselves. If the business has enough capital to do this, it can earn extra profits on the financing terms. Nonetheless, because of abuses, many consumer protection laws have been passed by both the federal and state governments.

Regulation Z

Two important federal laws regarding financing are called the *Truth in Lending Act* and the *Fair Credit Billing Act*. These are implemented by what is called *Regulation Z* (commonly known as *Reg. Z*), issued by the Board of Governors of the Federal Reserve System. (1 C.F.R., Vol. 12, p. 226.) This is a very complicated law, and some have said that no business can be sure to be in compliance with it.

The regulation covers all transactions in which four conditions are met:
1. credit is offered;
2. the offering of credit is regularly done;
3. there is a finance charge for the credit or there is a written agreement with more than four payments; and,
4. the credit is for personal, family, or household purposes.

It also covers credit card transactions where only the first two conditions are met. It applies to leases if the consumer ends up paying the full value and keeping the item leased. It does not apply to the following transactions:
◆ transactions with businesses or agricultural purposes;
◆ transactions with organizations such as corporations or the government;

- transactions of over $25,000 that are not secured by the consumer's dwelling;
- credit involving public utilities;
- credit involving securities or commodities; and,
- home fuel budget plans.

The way for a small business to avoid Reg. Z violations is to avoid transactions that meet the conditions or to make sure all transactions fall under the exceptions. For many businesses, this is easy. Instead of extending credit to customers, accept credit cards and let the credit card company extend the credit. However, if your customers usually do not have credit cards or if you are in a business that often extends credit, such as used car sales, you should consult a lawyer knowledgeable about Regulation Z or get a copy for yourself at **www.cardreport.com/laws/tila/tila.html**.

Collections

The *Fair Debt Collection Practices Act of 1977* bans the use of deception, harassment, and other unreasonable acts in the collection of debts. It has strict requirements whenever someone is collecting a debt for someone else. If you are in the collection business, you must get a copy of this law.

The Federal Trade Commission has issued some rules that prohibit deceptive representations, such as pretending to be in the motion picture industry, the government, or a credit bureau, or using questionnaires that do not say that they are for the purpose of collecting a debt. (C.F.R., Title 16, Ch. I, Part 237.)

Chapter 15:

Business Relations Law

At both the federal and state levels, there exist many laws regarding how businesses relate to one another. Some of the more important ones are discussed in this chapter.

The Uniform Commercial Code

The *Uniform Commercial Code* (UCC) is a set of laws regulating numerous aspects of doing business. A national group drafted this set of uniform laws to avoid having a patchwork of different laws around the fifty states. Although some states modified some sections of the laws, the code is basically the same in most of the states. Each chapter is concerned with a different aspect of commercial relations, such as sales, warranties, bank deposits, commercial paper, and bulk transfers.

Businesses that wish to know their rights in all types of transactions should obtain a copy of the UCC and become familiar with it. It is especially useful in transactions between merchants. However, the meaning is not always clear from reading the statutes.

Commercial Discrimination

The *Robinson-Patman Act of 1936* prohibits businesses from injuring competition by offering the same goods at different prices to different buyers. This means that the large chain stores should not be getting a better price than your small shop. It also requires that promotional allowances must be made on proportionally the same terms to all buyers.

As a small business, you may be a victim of Robinson-Patman Act violation, but fighting a much larger company in court would probably be too expensive for you. Your best bet, if an actual violation has occurred, would be to see if you could get the government to prosecute it. For more information on what constitutes a violation, see the Federal Trade Commission and the Department of Justice's joint site at **www.ftc.gov/bc/compguide**.

Restraining Trade

One of the earliest federal laws affecting business is the *Sherman Antitrust Act of 1890*. The purpose of the law was to protect competition in the marketplace by prohibiting monopolies.

Examples of some things that are prohibited are:
   ◆ agreements between competitors to sell at the same prices;
   ◆ agreements between competitors on how much will be sold or produced;
   ◆ agreements between competitors to divide up a market;
   ◆ refusing to sell one product without a second product; or,
   ◆ exchanging information among competitors, which results in similarity of prices.

As a small business, you will probably not be in a position to violate the Sherman Act, but you should be aware of it if a larger competitor tries to put you out of business. Fighting a much larger company in court would probably be too expensive for you, but if an actual violation has occurred, you might be able to get the government to prosecute it. For more information on what constitutes a violation, see the website by the Federal Trade Commission and the Department of Justice at **www.ftc.gov/bc/compguide**.

Intellectual Property Protection

As a business owner, you should know enough about intellectual property law to protect your own creations and to keep from violating the rights of others. *Intellectual property* is the product of human creativity, such as writings, designs, inventions, melodies, and processes. They are things that can be stolen without being physically taken. For example, if you write a book, someone can steal the words from your book without stealing a physical copy of it.

As the Internet grows, intellectual property is becoming more valuable. Business owners should take the action necessary to protect their companies' intellectual property. Additionally, business owners should know intellectual property law to be sure that they do not violate the rights of others. Even an unknowing violation of the law can result in stiff fines and penalties.

The following are the types of intellectual property and the ways to protect them.

Patent

A *patent* is protection given to new and useful inventions, discoveries, and designs. To be entitled to a patent, a work must be completely new and unobvious. A patent is granted to the first inventor who files for the patent. Once an invention is patented, no one else can make use of that invention, even if they discover it independently after a lifetime of research. A patent protects an invention for seventeen years; for designs, they are protected for fourteen years. Patents cannot be renewed. The patent application must clearly explain how to make the invention so that when the patent expires, others will be able to freely make and use the invention. Patents are registered with the *United States Patent and Trademark Office* (PTO). Examples of things that would be patentable would be mechanical devices or new drug formulas.

In recent years, patents have been used to protect computer programs and things such as business methods, including Amazon's one-click ordering. Few cases challenging these patents have gotten through the court system, so it is too early to tell if they will hold up. About half the patents that reach the Supreme Court are held to be invalid.

Copyright

A *copyright* is protection given to original works of authorship, such as written works, musical works, visual works, performance works, or computer software programs. A copyright exists from the moment of creation, but you cannot register a copyright until it has been fixed in tangible form. Also, you cannot copyright titles, names, or slogans. A copyright currently gives the author and his or her heirs exclusive right to the work for the life of the author plus seventy years.

Copyrights first registered before 1978 last for ninety-five years. (This was previously seventy-five years, but was extended twenty years to match the European system.) Copyrights are registered with the Register of Copyrights at the Library of Congress. Examples of works that would be copyrightable are books, paintings, songs, poems, plays, drawings, and films.

Trademark

A *trademark* is protection given to a name or symbol used to distinguish one person's goods or services from those of others. It can consist of letters, numerals, packaging, labeling, musical notes, colors, or a combination of these. If a trademark is used on services as opposed to goods, it is called a *service mark*.

A trademark lasts indefinitely if it is used continuously and renewed properly. Trademarks are registered with the United States Patent and Trademark Office and with individual states. (This is explained further in Chapter 3.) Examples of trademarks are the Chrysler name on automobiles, the red border on TIME magazine, and the shape of the Coca-Cola bottle.

Trade Secret

A *trade secret* is some information or process that provides a commercial advantage that is protected by keeping it a secret. Examples of trade secrets may be a list of successful distributors, the formula for Coca-Cola, or some unique source code in a computer program. Trade secrets are not registered anywhere—they are protected by the fact that they are not disclosed. They are protected only for as long as they are kept secret. If you independently discover the formula for Coca-Cola tomorrow, you can freely market it (but you cannot use the trademark "Coca-Cola" on your product to market it).

Unprotected Creations

Some things just cannot be protected—such things as ideas, systems, and discoveries are not allowed any protection under any law. If you have a great idea, such as selling packets of hangover medicine in bars, you cannot stop others from doing the same thing. If you invent a new medicine, you can patent it; if you pick a distinctive name for it, you can register it as a trademark; if you create a unique picture or instructions for the package, you can copyright them. However, you cannot stop others from using your basic business idea of marketing hangover medicine in bars.

Notice the subtle differences between the protective systems available. If you invent something two days after someone else does, you cannot even use it yourself if the other person has patented it. However, if you write the same poem as someone else and neither of you copied the other, both of you can copyright the poem. If you patent something, you can have the exclusive rights to it for the term of the patent, but you must disclose how others can make it after the patent expires. However, if you keep it a trade secret, you have exclusive rights as long as no one learns the secret.

Chapter 16:

Endless Laws

Every state and the federal government have numerous laws and rules that apply to every aspect of every type of business. There are even laws governing such things as fence posts, hosiery, rabbit raising, refund policies, frozen desserts, and advertising. Every business is affected by at least one of these laws.

Some activities are covered by both state and federal laws. In such cases, you must obey the stricter of the rules. In addition, more than one agency of the state or federal government may have rules governing your business. Each of these may have the power to investigate violations and impose fines or other penalties.

Penalties for violations of these laws can range from a warning to a criminal fine and even jail time. In some cases, employees can sue for damages. Recently, employees have been given awards of millions of dollars from employers who violated the law. Since ignorance of the law is no excuse, it is your duty to learn which laws apply to your business, or to risk these penalties.

Very few people in business know the laws that apply to their businesses. If you take the time to learn them, you can become an expert in your field, and avoid problems with regulators. You can also fight back if one of your competitors uses some illegal method to compete with you.

The laws and rules that affect the most businesses are explained in this section. Following that is a list of more specialized laws. You should read through this list and see which ones may apply to your business. Then, go to your public library or law library and read them. Some may not apply to your phase of the business, but if any of them do apply, you should make copies to keep on hand.

No one could possibly know all the rules that affect business, much less comply with them all. However, if you keep up with the important rules, you will stay out of trouble and have more chance of success.

Federal Laws

The federal laws that are most likely to affect small businesses are rules of the Federal Trade Commission (FTC). The FTC has some rules that affect many businesses, such as the rules about labeling, warranties, and mail order sales. Other rules affect only certain industries.

If you sell goods by mail, you should send for the FTC's booklet, *A Business Guide to the Federal Trade Commission's Mail Order Rule*. If you are going to be involved in a certain industry, such as those listed in this section, or using warranties or your own labeling, you should ask for their latest information on the subject. The address is:

Federal Trade Commission
600 Pennsylvania Avenue, NW
Washington, DC 20580

The rules of the FTC are contained in the Code of Federal Regulations (C.F.R.). Some of the industries covered include the following.

Industry	Part
Adhesive Compositions	235
Aerosol Products Used for Frosting Cocktail Glasses	417
Automobiles (New car fuel economy advertising)	259
Barber Equipment and Supplies	248
Binoculars	402
Business Opportunities and Franchises	436
Cigarettes	408
Decorative Wall Paneling	243
Dog and Cat Food	241
Dry Cell Batteries	403
Extension Ladders	418
Fallout Shelters	229
Feather and Down Products	253
Fiber Glass Curtains	413
Food (Games of Chance)	419
Funerals	453
Gasoline (Octane posting)	306
Gasoline	419
Greeting Cards	244
Home Entertainment Amplifiers	432
Home Insulation	460
Hosiery	22
Household Furniture	250
Jewelry	23
Ladies' Handbags	247
Law Books	256
Light Bulbs	409
Luggage and Related Products	24
Mail Order Insurance	234
Mail Order Merchandise	435
Men's and Boys' Tailored Clothing	412
Metallic Watch Band	19
Mirrors	21
Nursery	18
Ophthalmic Practices	456
Photographic Film and Film Processing	242
Private Vocational and Home Study Schools	254
Radiation Monitoring Instruments	232
Retail Food Stores (Advertising)	424
Shell Homes	230
Shoes	231
Sleeping Bags	400

Some other federal laws that affect businesses are as follows.

- *Alcohol Administration Act*
- *Child Protection and Toy Safety Act*
- *Clean Water Act*
- *Comprehensive Smokeless Tobacco Health Education Act*
- *Consumer Credit Protection Act*
- *Consumer Product Safety Act*
- *Energy Policy and Conservation Act*
- *Environmental Pesticide Control Act of 1972*
- *Fair Credit Reporting Act*
- *Fair Packaging and Labeling Act of 1966*
- *Flammable Fabrics Act*
- *Food, Drug, and Cosmetic Act*
- *Fur Products Labeling Act*
- *Hazardous Substances Act*
- *Hobby Protection Act*
- *Insecticide, Fungicide, and Rodenticide Act*
- *Magnuson-Moss Warranty Act*
- *Poison Prevention Packaging Act of 1970*
- *Solid Waste Disposal Act*
- *Textile Fiber Products Identification Act*
- *Toxic Substance Control Act*
- *Wool Products Labeling Act*
- *Nutrition Labeling and Education Act of 1990*
- *Food Safety Enforcement Enhancement Act of 1997*

State Laws

Since each state has its own laws, it would be impossible to list them all here. Instead, the following is a list of types of businesses in which a law may have been passed. Do additional research in your state to determine if any specialized law or rule has been passed that you must obey.

Adoption agencies
Adult congregate living facilities
Adult day care facilities
Adult foster home care
Air conditioning
Aircraft, pilots, and airports
Alcoholic beverages
Ambulance service contracts
Anatomical matter
Animals
Antifreeze
Aquaculture
Art and craft material
Auctions
Automobile racing
Bail bondsmen
Banking
Boiler safety
Bottles and boxes, markings
Boxing and fighting
Brake fluid
Budget planning
Buildings, radon resistance stds.
Burial contracts
Business opportunities
Cemeteries
Charitable solicitation
Citrus

Collections
Commissions merchants
Condominiums
Construction
Consumer finance
Cooperatives
Cosmetics
Counseling and psychotherapy
Crash parts
Credit cards
Credit service organizations
Dairies
Dance studios
Desserts, frozen
Dog racing and horse racing
Drinking water
Driving schools
Drugs
Eggs and poultry
Electrical
Electronic repair
Elevators, Escalators
Energy conservation standards
Equity exchanges
Explosives
Factory-built housing
Fence posts
Fences and livestock at large

Fiduciary funds
Fireworks
Food
Franchises
Frontons
Fruits and vegetables
Fuels, liquid
Future consumer services
Gambling and lotteries
Gas, liquefied petroleum
Gasoline and oil
Glass
Hazardous substances
Hazardous waste amnesty
Health care
Health studios
Home health agencies
Home improvement sales and fin.
Home solicitation sales
Honey
Horse sales, shows, exhibitions
Hospices
Hotels
Household products
Housing codes, state minimum
Identification cards
Insurance and service plans
Invention development
Land sales
Lasers and nonionizing radiation
Lead acid batteries
Legal services
Linen suppliers
Liquor

Livestock
Lodging
Marketing establishments
Meats
Mental health
Metal recyclers
Milk and milk products
Mining waste
Mobile homes
Money orders
Motion pictures
Motor vehicle lemon law
Motor vehicles
Multilevel marketing
Naval stores
Newsprint
Nursing homes
Obscene literature
Occupational therapists
Outdoor advertising
Outdoor theatres
Pari-mutuel wagering
Peanut marketing
Pest control
Photos of admission parks
Plants and nurseries
Plumbing
Private investigators
Prostitution
Pyramid schemes
Radiation
Radio and television repairs
Real estate sales
Rental housing

Restaurants
Sanitarians
Secondhand dealers
Securities transactions
Soybean marketing
Swimming and bathing places
Syrup
Telegraph and cable companies
Telemarketing
Telephone companies
Television picture tubes
Term papers, dissertations
Thermal efficiency standards
Timber and lumber
Time-shares
Tires
Tobacco
Tourist attraction
Tourist camps
Travel services
Sound and film, copying
Viticulture
Watches, used
Watermelon marketing
Weapons and firearms
Yacht or ship brokers

Chapter 17:

Bookkeeping and Accounting

It is beyond the scope of this book to explain all the intricacies of setting up a business's bookkeeping and accounting systems. However, it is important to realize that if you do not set up an understandable bookkeeping system, your business will undoubtedly fail.

Without accurate records of where your income is coming from and where it is going, you will be unable to increase your profits, lower your expenses, obtain needed financing, or make the right decisions in all areas of your business. The time to decide how you will handle your bookkeeping is when you open your business—not a year later when it is tax time.

Initial Bookkeeping

If you do not understand business taxation, you should pick up a good book on the subject, as well as the IRS tax guide for your type of business (proprietorship, partnership, corporation, or limited liability company).

The IRS tax book for small businesses is Publication 334, *Tax Guide for Small Businesses*. There are also instruction booklets for each type of business form, including Schedule C for proprietorships, Form 1120 or 1120S for C corporations and S corporations, and 1165 for partnerships and businesses that are taxed like partnerships (LLCs, LLPs).

Keep in mind that the IRS does not give you the best advice for saving on taxes and does not give you the other side of contested issues. For that, you need a private tax guide or advisor.

The most important thing to do is to set up your bookkeeping so that you can easily fill out your monthly, quarterly, and annual tax returns. The best way to do this is to get copies of the returns—not the totals that you will need to supply—and set up your bookkeeping system to group those totals.

For example, for a sole proprietorship, you will use Schedule C to report business income and expenses to the IRS at the end of the year. Use the categories on that form to sort your expenses. To make your job especially easy, every time you pay a bill, put the category number on the check.

Accountants

Most likely, your new business will not be able to afford hiring an accountant right away to handle your books. Do not be discouraged—doing them yourself will force you to learn about business accounting and taxation. The worst way to run a business is to know nothing about the tax laws and turn everything over to an accountant at the end of the year to find out what is due.

You should know the basics of tax law before making basic decisions, such as whether to buy or rent equipment or premises. You should understand accounting so you can time your financial affairs appropriately. If your business needs to buy supplies, inventory, or equipment, and provides goods or services throughout the year, you need to at least have a basic understanding of the system within which you are working.

Once you can afford an accountant, you should weigh the cost against your time and the risk that you will make an error. Even if you think you know enough to do your own corporate tax return, you should still take it to an accountant one year to see if you have been missing any deductions. You might decide that the money saved is worth the cost of the accountant's services.

Computer Programs

Today, every business should keep its books by computer. There are inexpensive programs, such as Quicken, that can instantly provide you with reports of your income and expenses, as well as the right figures to plug into your tax returns.

Most programs even offer a tax program each year that will take all of your information and print it out on the current year's tax forms.

Tax Tips

The following are a few tax tips for small businesses that will help you save money.

◆ Usually, when you buy equipment for a business, you must amortize the cost over several years. That is, you do not deduct it all when you buy it, but instead, take, say, 25% of the cost off your taxes each year for four years. (The time is determined by the theoretical usefulness of the item.) However, small businesses are allowed to write off the entire cost of a limited amount of items under Internal Revenue Code (I.R.C.) Sec. 179. If you have income to shelter, use it.

◆ Owners of S corporations do not have to pay Social Security or Medicare taxes on the part of their profits that is not considered salary. As long as you pay yourself a reasonable salary, other money you take out is not subject to these taxes.

◆ You should not neglect to deposit withholding taxes for your own salary or profits. Besides being a large sum to come up with at once in April, there are penalties that must be paid for failure to deposit withholding taxes.

◆ Do not fail to keep track of and remit your employees' withholding. You will be personally liable for them even if you are a corporation.

◆ If you keep track of the use of your car for business, you can deduct 44.5¢ per mile (this may go up or down each year—check with the IRS for current rates). If you use your car for business a considerable amount of the time, you may be able to depreciate it.

- ◆ If your business is a corporation and if you designate the stock as Section 1244 stock, then if the business fails you are able to get a much better deduction for the loss.
- ◆ By setting up a retirement plan, you can exempt up to 20% of your salary from income tax. However, do not use money you might need later. There are penalties for taking it out of the retirement plan.
- ◆ When you buy things that will be resold or made into products that will be resold, you do not have to pay sales taxes on those purchases.

Chapter 18:

Paying Taxes

The federal government levies many different types of taxes on individuals and businesses. It is very important that you consult an accountant or attorney to properly comply with and take advantage of the incredibly complex federal tax code and regulations. This chapter discusses several of the most important federal taxes that will most likely affect your new business.

Income Tax

The manner in which each type of business pays taxes is as follows.

Proprietorship

A proprietor reports profits and expenses on Schedule C attached to the usual Form 1040, and pays tax on all of the net income of the business. Each quarter, Form ES-1040 must be filed, along with payment of one-quarter of the amount of income tax and Social Security taxes estimated to be due for the year.

Partnership

The partnership files a return showing the income and expenses, but pays no tax. Each partner is given a form showing his or her share of the profits or losses, and reports these on Schedule E of Form 1040. Each quarter, Form ES-1040 must be filed by each partner along with payment of one-quarter of the amount of income tax and Social Security taxes estimated to be due for the year.

C Corporation

A regular corporation is a separate taxpayer, and pays tax on its profits after deducting all expenses, including officers' salaries. If dividends are distributed, they are paid out of after-tax dollars, and the shareholders pay tax a second time when they receive the dividends. If a corporation needs to accumulate money for investment, it may be able to do so at lower tax rates than the shareholders. However, if all profits will be distributed to shareholders, the double taxation may be excessive unless all income is paid as salaries. C corporations file Form 1120.

S Corporation

A small corporation has the option of being taxed like a partnership. If Form 2553 is filed by the corporation and accepted by the Internal Revenue Service, the S corporation will only file an informational return listing profits and expenses. Then, each shareholder will be taxed on a proportional share of the profits (or be able to deduct a proportional share of the losses). Unless a corporation will make a large profit that will not be distributed, S status is usually best in the beginning. An S corporation files Form 1120S and distributes Form K-1 to each shareholder. If any money is taken out by a shareholder that is not listed as wages subject to withholding, then the shareholder will usually have to file Form ES-1040 each quarter along with payment of the estimated withholding on the withdrawals.

Limited Liability Companies and Partnerships

Limited liability companies and professional limited liability companies are allowed by the IRS to elect to be taxed either as a partnership or a corporation. To make this election, you file Form 8832, *Entity Classification Election*, with the IRS.

Tax Workshops and Booklets

The IRS conducts workshops to inform businesses about the tax laws. (Do not expect an in-depth study of the loopholes.) For more information, contact your local IRS branch for seminar times and locations. If you prefer to just read the manual for the workshop, which is IRS Publication 1066, you can download it from their website at **www.irs.gov**.

Withholding, Social Security, and Medicare Taxes

If you need basic information on business tax returns, the IRS publishes a rather large booklet that answers most questions and is available free of charge. Call or write them and ask for Publication 334. If you have any questions, look up their toll-free number in the phone book under "United States Government/Internal Revenue Service." If you want more creative answers and tax-saving information, you should find a good local accountant. To get started, you will need to be familiar with the following:

- employer identification number;
- Employee's Withholding Allowance Certificate;
- federal tax deposit coupons;
- electronic filing;
- Estimated Tax Payment Voucher;
- employer's quarterly tax return;
- Wage and Tax Statement;
- Form 1099 Miscellaneous; and,
- earned income credit.

Employer Identification Number

If you are a sole proprietor with no employees, you can use your Social Security number for your business. If you are a corporation, a partnership, or a proprietorship with employees, you must obtain an *employer identification number*. This is done by filing the APPLICATION FOR EMPLOYER IDENTIFICATION NUMBER (**IRS FORM SS-4**). (See the CD-ROM for a blank version of this form.) It usually takes a week or two to receive. You will need this number to open bank accounts for the business, so you should file this form a soon as you decide to go into business.

Employee's Withholding Allowance Certificate

You must have each employee fill out an Employee's Withholding Allowance Certificate (IRS Form W-4) to calculate the amount of federal taxes to be deducted and to obtain their Social Security numbers. (Visit **www.irs.gov** for the most recent version, as it changes annually. The number of allowances on this form is used with IRS Circular E, Publication 15, to figure out the exact deductions.)

Federal Tax Deposit Coupons

After taking withholdings from employees' wages, you must deposit them at a bank that is authorized to accept such funds. If at the end of any month you have over $1,000 in withheld taxes, including your contribution to FICA (Social Security and Medicare), you must make a deposit prior to the 15th of the following month. If on the 3rd, 7th, 11th, 15th, 19th, 22nd, or 25th of any month you have over $3,000 in withheld taxes, you must make a deposit within three banking days.

Electronic Filing

Each year, the IRS requires a few more forms to be filed electronically or over the telephone. When you receive your paper filing forms from the IRS, they will include your options for filing electronically or by telephone. In some cases, electronic filing may save time, but if your business is small and most of your numbers are zeros, it may be faster to mail in the paper forms.

Estimated Tax Payment Voucher

Sole proprietors and partners usually take draws from their businesses without the formality of withholding. However, they are still required to make deposits of income and FICA taxes each quarter. If more than $500 is due in April on a person's 1040 form, then not enough money was withheld each quarter and a penalty is assessed, unless the person falls into an exception. The quarterly withholding is submitted on Form 1040-ES on January 15th, April 15th, June 15th, and September 15th each year. If these days fall on a weekend, the due date is the following Monday. The worksheet with Estimated Tax Payment Voucher (Form 1040-ES) can be used to determine the amount to pay. (See **www.irs.gov** for this form.)

NOTE: *One of the exceptions to the rule is that if you withhold the same amount as last year's tax bill, then you do not have to pay a penalty. This is usually a lot easier than filling out the 1040-ES worksheet.*

Employer's Quarterly Tax Return

Each quarter, you must file Form 941, reporting your federal withholding and FICA taxes. If you owe more than $1,000 at the end of a quarter, you are required to make a deposit at the end of any month that you have $1,000 in withholding.

The deposits are made to the Federal Reserve Bank or an authorized financial institution on Form 501. Most banks are authorized to accept deposits. If you owe more than $3,000 for any month, you must make a deposit at any point in the month in which you owe $3,000. After you file Form SS-4, the 941 forms will be sent to you automatically if you checked the box saying that you expect to have employees.

Wage and Tax Statement

At the end of each year, you are required to issue a W-2 Form to each employee. This form shows the amount of wages paid to the employee during the year, as well as the amounts withheld for taxes, Social Security, Medicare, and other purposes.

Form 1099 Miscellaneous

If you pay at least $600 to a person other than an employee (such as independent contractors), you are required to file a Form 1099-MISC for that person. Along with the 1099s, you must file a Form 1096, which is a summary sheet of all the 1099s you issued.

Many people are not aware of this law and fail to file these forms, but they are required for such things as services, royalties, rents, awards, and prizes that you pay to individuals (but not corporations). The rules for this are quite complicated, so you should either obtain Package 1099 from the IRS or consult your accountant.

Earned Income Credit

Persons who are not liable to pay income tax may have the right to a check from the government because of the *earned income credit*. You are required to notify your employees of this. You can satisfy this requirement with one of the following:

- ◆ a W-2 Form with the notice on the back;
- ◆ a substitute for the W-2 Form with the notice on it;
- ◆ a copy of Notice 797; or,
- ◆ a written statement with the wording from Notice 797.

A Notice 797 can be downloaded from the IRS website at **www.irs.gov/pub/irs-pdf/n797.pdf**.

Excise Taxes

Excise taxes are taxes on certain activities or items. Some of the things that are subject to federal excise taxes are tobacco and alcohol, gasoline, tires and inner tubes, some trucks and trailers, firearms, ammunition, bows, arrows, fishing equipment, the use of highway vehicles of over 55,000 pounds, aircraft, wagering, telephone and teletype services, coal, hazardous wastes, and vaccines. If you are involved with any of these, you should obtain from IRS Publication 510, *Information on Excise Taxes.*

Unemployment Compensation Tax

You must pay federal unemployment taxes if you paid wages of $1,500 in any quarter, or if you had at least one employee for twenty calendar weeks. The federal tax amount is 0.8% of the first $7,000 of wages paid each employee. If more than $100 is due by the end of any quarter (if you paid $12,500 in wages for the quarter), then Form 508 must be filed with an authorized financial institution or the Federal Reserve Bank in your area. You will receive Form 508 when you obtain your employer identification number.

At the end of each year, you must file Form 940 or Form 940EZ. This is your annual report of federal unemployment taxes. You will receive an original form from the IRS.

State Taxes

Each state will have a variety of state tax requirements you will have to pay. Check with your state department of revenue, or similar agency, to learn your state's requirements. See Appendix D for a list of state departments of revenue.

Glossary

A

acceptance. Agreeing to the terms of an offer and creating a contract.

affirmative action. Hiring an employee to achieve a balance in the workplace, and avoid existing or continuing discrimination based on minority status.

alien. A person who is not a citizen of the country.

articles of incorporation. The document that sets forth the organization of a corporation.

B

bait advertising. Offering a product for sale with the intention of selling another product.

bulk sales. Selling substantially all of a company's inventory.

C

C corporation. A corporation that pays taxes on its profits.

collections. The collection of money owed to a business.

common law. Laws that are determined in court cases rather than statutes.

consideration. The exchange of value or promises in a contract.

contract. An agreement between two or more parties.

copyright. Legal protection given to original works of authorship.

corporation. An artificial person that is set up to conduct a business owned by shareholders, and run by officers and directors.

D

deceptive pricing. Pricing goods or services in a manner intended to deceive the customers.

discrimination. The choosing among various options based on their characteristics. It is illegal to use discriminatory hiring practices.

domain name. The address of a website.

E

employee. Person who works for another under that person's control and direction.

endorsements. Positive statements about goods or services.

excise tax. A tax paid on the sale or consumption of goods or services.

express warranty. A specific guarantee of a product or service.

F

fictitious name. A name used by a business that is not its personal or legal name.

G

general partnership. A business that is owned by two or more persons.

goods. Items of personal property.

guarantee. A promise of quality of a good or service.

I

implied warranty. A guarantee of a product or service that is not specifically made, but can be implied from the circumstances of the sale.

independent contractor. Person who works for another as a separate business, not as an employee.

intangible property. Personal property that does not have physical presence, such as the ownership interest in a corporation.

intellectual property. Legal rights to the products of the mind, such as writings, musical compositions, formulas, and designs.

L

liability. The legal responsibility to pay for an injury.

limited liability company. An entity recognized as a legal person that is set up to conduct a business owned and run by members.

limited liability partnership. An entity recognized as a legal person that is set up to conduct a business owned and run by members that is set up for professionals, such as attorneys or doctors.

limited partnership. A business that is owned by two or more persons, of which one or more is liable for the debts of the business, and one or more has no liability for the debts.

limited warranty. A guarantee covering certain aspects of a good or service.

M

merchant. A person who is in business.

merchant's firm offer. An offer by a business made under specific terms.

N

nonprofit corporation. An entity recognized as a legal person that is set up to run an operation in which none of the profits are distributed to controlling members.

O

occupational license. A government-issued permit to transact business.

offer. A proposal to enter into a contract.

overtime. Hours worked in excess of forty hours in one week, or eight hours in one day.

P

partnership. A business formed by two or more persons.

patent. Protection given to inventions, discoveries, and designs.

personal property. Any type of property other than land and the structures attached to it.

pierce the corporate veil. When a court ignores the structure of a corporation and holds its owners responsible for its debts or liabilities.

professional association. An entity recognized as a legal person that is set up to conduct a business of professionals, such as attorneys or doctors.

proprietorship. A business that is owned by one person.

R

real property. Land and the structures attached to it.

resident alien. A person who is not a citizen of a country, but who may legally reside and work there.

S

S corporation. A corporation in which the profits are taxed to the shareholders.

sale on approval. Selling an item with the agreement that it may be brought back and the sale cancelled.

sale or return. An agreement whereby goods are to be purchased or returned to the vendor.

securities. Interests in a business, such as stocks or bonds.

sexual harassment.   Activity that causes an employee to feel or be sexually threatened.

shares. Units of stock in a corporation.

statute of frauds. Law that requires certain contracts to be in writing.

stock. Ownership interests in a corporation.

sublease. An agreement to rent premises from an existing tenant.

T

tangible property. Physical personal property, such as desks and tables.

trade secret. Commercially valuable information or process that is protected by being kept a secret.

trademark. A name or symbol used to identify the source of goods or services.

U

unemployment compensation. Payments to a former employee who was terminated from a job for a reason not based on his or her fault.

usury. Charging an interest rate higher than that allowed by law.

W

withholding. Money taken out of an employee's salary and remitted to the government.

workers' compensation. Insurance program to cover injuries or deaths of employees.

Appendix A:

Business Start-Up Checklist

❏ Make your plan
    ❏ Obtain and read all relevant publications on your type of business
    ❏ Obtain and read all laws and regulations affecting your business
    ❏ Calculate whether your plan will produce a profit
    ❏ Plan your sources of capital
    ❏ Plan your sources of goods or services
    ❏ Plan your marketing efforts
❏ Choose your business name
    ❏ Check other business names and trademarks
    ❏ Register your name, trademark, etc.
❏ Choose the business form
    ❏ Prepare and file organizational papers
    ❏ Prepare and file fictitious name if necessary
❏ Choose the location
    ❏ Check competitors
    ❏ Check zoning
❏ Obtain necessary licenses
    ❏ City
    ❏ County
    ❏ State
    ❏ Federal

❏ Choose a bank
  ❏ Checking account
  ❏ Credit card processing
  ❏ Loans
❏ Obtain necessary insurance
  ❏ Automobile
  ❏ Hazard
  ❏ Health
  ❏ Liability
  ❏ Life/Disability
  ❏ Workers' compensation
❏ File necessary federal tax registrations
❏ File necessary state tax registrations
❏ Set up a bookkeeping system
❏ Plan your hiring
  ❏ Obtain required posters
  ❏ Obtain or prepare employment application
  ❏ Obtain new hire tax forms
  ❏ Prepare employment policies
  ❏ Determine compliance with health and safety laws
❏ Plan your opening
  ❏ Obtain all necessary equipment and supplies
  ❏ Obtain all necessary inventory
  ❏ Do all necessary marketing and publicity
  ❏ Obtain all necessary forms and agreements
  ❏ Prepare your company policies on refunds, exchanges, returns, etc.

Appendix B:

SBA District Offices

This appendix contains the district offices of the Small Business Administration (SBA) in each state. You can find further information at **www.sba.gov**.

ALASKA
Anchorage District Office
510 L Street
Suite 310
Anchorage, AK 99501
907-271-4022

ALABAMA
Birmingham District Office
801 Tom Martin Drive
Suite #201
Birmingham, AL 35211
205-290-7101

ARKANSAS
Little Rock District Office
2120 Riverfront Drive
Suite 250
Little Rock, AR 72202
501-324-7379

ARIZONA
Phoenix District Office
2828 North Central Avenue
Suite 800
Phoenix, AZ 85004
602-745-7200

CALIFORNIA
Fresno District Office
2719 North Air Fresno Drive
Suite 200
Fresno, CA 93727
559-487-5791

Los Angeles District Office
330 North Brand
Suite 1200
Glendale, CA 91203
818-552-3215

Sacramento District Office
650 Capitol Mall
Suite 7-500
Sacramento, CA 95814
916-930-3700

San Diego District Office
550 West C Street
Suite 550
San Diego, CA 92101
619-557-7250

San Francisco District Office
455 Market Street
6th Floor
San Francisco, CA 94105
415-744-6820

Santa Ana District Office
200 W Santa Ana Boulevard
Suite 700
Santa Ana, CA 92701
714-550-7420

COLORADA

Denver District Office
721 19th Street
Suite 426
Denver, CO 80202
303-844-2607

CONNECTICUT

Hartford District Office
330 Main Street
Second Floor
Hartford, CT 06106
860-240-4700

DISTRICT OF COLUMBIA

Washington Metropolitan Area District
Office
740 15th Street NW
Suite 300
Washington, D.C. 20005
202-272-0345

DELEWARE

Wilmington District Office
1007 North Orange Street
Suite 1120
Wilmington, DE 19801
302-573-6294

FLORIDA

Jacksonville District Office
7825 Baymeadows Way
Suite 100B
Jacksonville, FL 32256
904-443-1900

Miami District Office
100 South Biscayne Blvd
7th Floor
Miami, FL 33131
305-536-5521

GEORGIA

Georgia District Office
233 Peachtree Street, NE
Suite 1900
Atlanta, GA 30303
404-331-0100

GUAM

Guam District Office
400 Route 8
Suite 302
Mongmong, GU 96927
671-472-7419

HAWAII

Honolulu District Office
300 Ala Moana Boulevard
Room 2-235
Box 50207
Honolulu, Hawaii 96850
808-541-2990

IOWA

Cedar Rapids District Office
2750 1st Avenue NE
Suite 350
Cedar Rapids, IA 52402
319-362-6405

Des Moines District Office
210 Walnut Street
Room 749
Des Moines, IA 50309
515-284-4422

IDAHO

Boise District Office
380 East Parkcenter Boulevard
Suite 330
Boise, ID 83706
208-334-1696

ILLINOIS

Chicago District Office
500 West Madison Street
Suite 1250
Chicago, IL 60661
312-353-4528

Springfield District Office
3330 Ginger Creek Road
Suite B
Springfield, IL 62711
217-793-5020

INDIANA

Indianapolis District Office
8500 Keystone Crossing
Suite 400
Indianapolis, IN 46240
317-226-7272

KANSAS

Wichita District Office
271 W 3rd Street, N
Suite 2500
Wichita, KS 67202
316-269-6616

KENTUCKY

Louisville District Office
600 Dr. Martin Luther King Jr Place
Room 188
Louisville, KY 40202
502-582-5971

LOUISIANA

New Orleans District Office
365 Canal Street
Suite 2820
New Orleans, LA 70130
504-589-6685

MASSACHUSETTS

Boston District Office
10 Causeway Street
Room 265
Boston, MA 02222
617-565-5590

MARYLAND

Baltimore District Office
City Crescent Building
6th Floor
10 South Howard Street
Baltimore, MD 21201
410-962-4392

MAINE

Augusta District Office
Edmund S. Muskie Federal Building
Room 512
68 Sewall Street
Augusta, ME 04330
207-622-8274

MICHIGAN

Detroit District Office
477 Michigan Avenue
Suite 515, McNamara Building
Detroit, MI 48226
313-226-6075

MINNESOTA

Minneapolis District Office
100 North Sixth Street
Suite 210-C Butler Square
Minneapolis, MN 55403
612-370-2324

MISSOURI

Kansas City District Office
1000 Walnut
Suite 500
Kansas City, MO 64106
816-426-4900

St. Louis District Office
200 North Broadway
Suite 1500
St. Louis, MO 63102
314-539-6600

MISSISSIPPI

Jackson District Office
AmSouth Bank Plaza
210 East Capitol Street
Suite 900
Jackson, MS 39201
601-965-4378

Gulfport Branch Office
Gulf Coast Business Technology
  Center
1636 Popps Ferry Road
Suite 229
Biloxi, MS 39532
228-863-4449

MONTANA

Helena District Office
10 West 15th Street
Suite 1100
Helena, MT 59626
406-441-1081

NORTH CAROLINA

Charlotte District Office
6302 Fairview Road
Suite 300
Charlotte, NC 28210
704-344-6563

NORTH DAKOTA

Fargo District Office
657 2nd Avenue North
Room 218
P.O. Box 3086
Fargo, ND 58108
701-239-5131

NEBRASKA

Omaha District Office
11145 Mill Valley Road
Omaha, NE 68154
402-221-4691

NEW HAMPSHIRE

Concord District Office
JC Cleveland Federal Building
55 Pleasant Street
Suite 3101
Concord, NH 03301
603-225-1400

NEW JERSEY

New Jersey District Office
Two Gateway Center
15th Floor
Newark, NJ 07102
973-645-2434

NEW MEXICO

Albuquerque District Office
625 Silver SW
Suite 320
Albuquerque, NM 87102
505-248-8225

NEVADA

Las Vegas District Office
400 South 4th Street
Suite 250
Las Vegas, NV 89101
702-388-6611

NEW YORK

Buffalo District Office
Niagara Center
130 South Elmwood Avenue
Suite 540
Buffalo, NY 14202
716-551-4301

New York District Office
26 Federal Plaza
Suite 3100
New York, NY 10278
212-264-4354

Syracuse District Office
401 South Salina Street
5th Floor
Syracuse, NY 13202
315-471-9393

OHIO

Cleveland District Office
1350 Euclid Avenue
Suite 211
Cleveland, OH 44115
216-522-4180

Columbus District Office
401 North Front Street
Suite 200
Columbus, OH 43215
614-469-6860

OKLAHOMA

Oklahoma City District Office
Federal Building
301 NW 6th Street
Oklahoma City, OK 73102
405-609-8000

OREGON

Portland District Office
601 SW Second Avenue
Suite 950
Portland, OR 97204
503-326-2682

PENNSYLVANIA

Philadelphia District Office
Robert N.C. Nix Federal Building
900 Market Street
5th Floor
Philadelphia, PA 19107
215-580-2722
Pittsburgh District Office
411 Seventh Avenue
Suite 1450
Pittsburgh, PA 15219
412-395-6560

PUERTO RICO

Puerto Rico District Office
252 Ponce de Leon Avenue
Citibank Tower
Suite 200
San Juan, PR 00918
787-766-5572
800-669-8049

U.S. VIRGIN ISLANDS

St. Croix Post of Duty
Sunny Isle Professional Building
Suites 5 & 6
St. Croix, USVI 00830
340-778-5380
800-669-8049
340-778-1102

RHODE ISLAND

Providence District Office
380 Westminster Street
Room 511
Providence, RI 02903
401-528-4561

SOUTH CAROLINA

Columbia District Office
1835 Assembly Street
Room 1425
Columbia, SC 29201
803-765-5377

SOUTH DAKOTA

Sioux Falls District Office
2329 North Career Avenue
Suite 105
Sioux Falls, SD 57107
605-330-4243

TENNESSEE

Nashville District Office
50 Vantage Way
Suite 201
Nashville, TN 37228
615-736-5881

TEXAS

Dallas/Fort Worth District Office
4300 Amon Carter Boulevard
Suite 114
Fort Worth, TX 76155
817-684-5500

El Paso District Office
10737 Gateway West
El Paso, TX 79935
915-633-7001

Dallas/Fort Worth District Office
4300 Amon Carter Boulevard
Suite 114
Fort Worth, TX 76155
817-684-5500

Harlingen District Office
222 East Van Buren Avenue
Suite 500
Harlingen, TX 78550
956-427-8533

Houston District Office
8701 South Gessner Drive
Suite 1200
Houston, TX 77074
713-773-6500

Lubbock District Office
1205 Texas Avenue
Room 408
Lubbock, TX 79401
806-472-7462

San Antonio District Office
17319 San Pedro
Suite 200
San Antonio, TX 78232
210-403-5900

UTAH

Salt Lake City District Office
125 South State Street
Room 2227
Salt Lake City, UT 84138
801-524-3209

VIRGINIA

Richmond District Office
The Federal Building
400 North 8th Street
Suite 1150
Richmond, VA 23219-4829
804-771-2400

VERMONT

Montpelier District Office
87 State Street
Room 205
Montpelier, VT 05601
802-828-4422

WASHINGTON

Seattle District Office
2401 Fourth Avenue
Suite 450
Seattle, WA 98121
206-553-7310

Spokane Branch Office
801 West Riverside Avenue
Suite 200
Spokane, WA   99201
509-353-2800

WISCONSIN

Madison District Office
740 Regent Street
Suite 100
Madison, WI 53715
608-441-5263

Milwaukee District Office
310 West Wisconsin Avenue
Room 400
Milwaukee, WI 53203
414-297-3941

WEST VIRGINIA

Clarksburg District Office
320 West Pike Street
Suite 330
Clarksburg, WV 26301
304-623-5631

WYOMING

Casper District Office
100 East B Street
Federal Building
Room 4001
P.O. Box 44001
Casper, WY 82602
307-261-6500
800-776-9144 Ext. 1

Appendix C:

LLC & Corporation Contact Information and Special Requirements

The following pages contain a listing of each state's limited liability company laws and fees. Because the laws are constantly being changed by state legislatures, you should call before filing your papers to confirm the fees and other requirements. The phone numbers are provided for each state.

With the continued growth of the Internet, more and more state corporation divisions are making their forms, fees, and requirements available online. Some states have downloadable forms available, and some even allow you to search their entire database from the comfort of your home or office.

The current websites at the time of publication of this book are included for each state. However, the sites change constantly, so you may need to look a little deeper if your state's site has changed its address.

NOTE: *Not all states have a sample form.*

Alabama

Secretary of State
Corporations Division
P.O. Box 5616
Montgomery, AL 36103-5616
334-242-5324

Website:
www.sos.state.al.us/business/
    corporations.cfm

LIMITED LIABILITY COMPANY

WHAT MUST BE FILED:

You must file the original and two copies of the Articles of Organization in the county where the LLC's registered office is located. The probate court judge will receive and record the original Articles. Within thirty days of filing, a completed report (provided by the secretary of state with the filing package) must be filed with the Judge of Probate ($5 filing fee).

ARTICLES OF ORGANIZATION SPECIAL REQUIREMENTS:

The Articles must set forth the rights, terms, and conditions to admit additional members, and, if given, the right by remaining members to continue business after dissociation.

STATUTES:

Code of Alabama, Title 10, Chapter 12, Alabama Limited Liability Company Act.

CORPORATION

WHAT MUST BE FILED:

You need to file the original and two copies of the Articles of Corporation in the county where the corporation's registered office is located.

ARTICLES REQUIREMENTS:

The minimum requirements for the Articles are as follows:

- the name of the corporation
- the period of duration
- the purpose of the corporation
- any provisions for the regulation of the internal affairs (including final liquidation)
- local and mailing address
- number of the directors constituting the initial board of directors and names and addresses of the initial directors
- name and address of each incorporator

STATUTE: Alabama Code 10-3A-1 to 225

Alaska

Department of Commerce and
   Economic Development
Division of B.S.C.
Attention: Corporation Section
P.O. Box 110808
Juneau, AK 99811-0808
907-465-2530
Fax: 907-465-3257

Website:
www.commerce.state.ak.us/bsc/home.htm

LIMITED LIABILITY COMPANY

WHAT MUST BE FILED:

An original and an exact copy of the fill-in-the-blank Articles of Organization. The Articles should contain a statement that they are being filed under the provisions of the Alaska Limited Liability Act.

ARTICLES OF ORGANIZATION SPECIAL REQUIREMENTS:

The purpose of the LLC must be characterized with at least two S.I.C. code numbers which are listed in the chart on the next page.

STATUTES:

Alaska Statutes, Title 10, beginning with Section 50.010, Alaska Limited Liability Act.

CORPORATION

WHAT MUST BE FILED:

Print or type your documents in dark, legible print and file two copies of the Articles of Incorporation. Computer print must be high resolution, laser print quality, suitable for microfilming. Make sure your documents bear the original signatures and are both notarized. Enclose the filing fee. One copy will be returned to you for your records. Paper must be no larger than 8 by 11 inches.

ARTICLES REQUIREMENTS:

You must state the names, telephone numbers, and addresses of your initial (first) board of directors in Article 6. In Alaska there must be at least three incorporators who must be natural persons at least 19 years old. Enter the names and (business) addresses of these incorporators in Article 7. Make sure that your Articles are notarized. The Articles should contain a statement that they are being filed under the provisions of the Alaska Nonprofit Corporation Act (AS 10.20).

- the name of the corporation
- the period of duration, which may be perpetual
- the purpose or purposes for which the corporation is organized
- any provisions for the regulation of the internal affairs (including final liquidation)
- physical address of its initial registered office and the name of its initial registered agent
- number of the directors constituting the initial board of directors and names and addresses of persons who are to serve as the initial directors
- the name and address of each incorporator

STATUTE: Alaska Statutes, Section 10.06.208-210

Arizona

Arizona Corporation Commission
1300 West Washington
Phoenix, AZ 85007-2929
602-542-3026
800-345-5819 (Arizona residents only)
or
400 West Congress
Tucson, AZ 85701-1347
520-628-6560

Website:
www.cc.state.az.us/corp/index.htm

LIMITED LIABILITY COMPANY

WHAT MUST BE FILED:

The original and one copy of the Articles of Organization must be filed with the Corporation Commission, copies will be returned if all requirements have been satisfied. DOMESTIC companies must publish a Notice of Filing. Within sixty days after filing, three consecutive publications of the Articles of Organization must be published in a newspaper of general circulation where the LLC has its place of business. Within ninety days after filing, an Affidavit evidencing the publication must also be filed with the Commission. This Affidavit will be supplied by the newspaper.

ARTICLES OF ORGANIZATION SPECIAL REQUIREMENTS:

The LLC must have a registered office and a statutory agent at a street address. The agent must sign the Articles or provide a consent to acceptance of appointment.

STATUTES:

Title 29, Chapter 4, Arizona Statutes (Arizona Limited Liability Company Act).

CORPORATION

WHAT MUST BE FILED:

Complete your Articles and file the original and two copies. Also fill in the Certificate of Disclosure and attach it to your Articles. Enclose the filing fee. After filing your Articles must be published within 60 days in a newspaper of general circulation in the county of the place of business in Arizona. There must be three consecutive publications of a copy of the approved Articles. Within 90 days of filing an affidavit evidencing the publication must be filed with the Commission.

ARTICLES REQUIREMENTS:

Enter one of the specific valid purposes for which a nonprofit corporation may be formed in Article 3.

In Article 5 and 6 you must enter the applicable Section number of of the IRS code under which your corporation plans to organize. Contact your local IRS office to obtain these numbers.

In Article 8 enter the name and business address of your initial statutory agent. This statutory agent has to sign the Articles on the bottom of the page.

Also complete your Certificate of Disclosure that has to be filed with your Articles. It contains information about your officers, directors, and anyone involved in the corporation.

STATUTE: Arizona Revised Statutes, Section 10-2300

Arkansas

Secretary of State
Corporation Division
State Capitol
Room 256
Little Rock, AR 72201
501-682-5078
888-233-0325
  (outside of the Little Rock area)
Website:
www.sosweb.state.ar.us/
  corp_ucc_business.html

LIMITED LIABILITY COMPANY

WHAT MUST BE FILED:

File two copies of Articles of Organization. A file stamped copy will be returned to you after filing has been completed. Also file one copy of Limited Liability Company Franchise Tax registration form.

ARTICLES OF ORGANIZATION SPECIAL REQUIREMENTS:

Registered agent must sign acknowledgment and acceptance of the appointment.

If the management of the company is vested in managers this must be stated in the articles.

STATUTES:

Small Business Entity Tax Pass Through Act, Act 1003 of 1993, Ark. Code Annotated, beginning with Section 4-32-101.

CORPORATION

WHAT MUST BE FILED:

Complete both copies of the fill-in-the-blanks Articles and file them with the Secretary of State. Make sure that the Articles are signed by all incorporators.

ARTICLES REQUIREMENTS:

The minimum requirements for the Articles are as follows:

- the name of the corporation
- the determination whether the corporation shall be a public-benefit, a mutual-benefit or a religious corporation
- a statement whether or not the corporation will have members
- if applicable, provisions regarding the distribution of assets on dissolution
- the street address and the name of the corporation's initial registered office
- the address and signature of each incorporator

STATUTE: Arkansas Code, Title 4, Sec. 28-206

California

Secretary of State
  Corporations Division
1500 11th Street
Sacramento, CA 95814
916-657-5448
or
Statement of Information Unit
  (filings only)
P.O. Box 944230
Sacramento, CA 94244-2300

Website:
www.ss.ca.gov/business/business.htm

LIMITED LIABILITY COMPANY

WHAT MUST BE FILED:

File only the original executed document together with the filing fee. A certified copy of the original document will be returned to you after filing.

ARTICLES OF ORGANIZATION SPECIAL REQUIREMENTS:

The Articles must be filed on California form LLC-1 and not a substitute. A form is on the next page.

STATUTES:

California Corporation Code, Section 17000-17062 (Beverly-Killea Limited Liability Company Act).

CORPORATION

WHAT MUST BE FILED:

Draft your own Articles accordingly to the applicable sample Articles provided by the state. The documents must be typed in black ink on one side of the paper only. To avoid the initial annual franchise tax of $800 complete the application form for exemption from franchise tax (form 3500), enclose all attachments called for in the instructions, and file this application together with the original and four copies of your Articles. Also enclose the $25 application filing fee, the state filing fee, and a self-addressed envelope. The Secretary of State will certify two copies without charge. Any additional copies will be certified upon request and payment of $8 per copy.

ARTICLES REQUIREMENTS:

Articles must have the following minimum contents:

- the corporate name
- the general purpose (Mutual Benefit Corporation, Public Benefit Corporation, Religious Corporation) and the specific purpose of the corporation
- name and California street address of the initial agent (post office box alone is not acceptable)
- signature and typed name (directly below the signature) of at least one incorporator
- if directors are stated in the Articles, each named person must acknowledge and sign the Articles
- special statements required to be included in the Articles to get the tax exemption (only where applicable—please contact the Franchise Tax Board under the address typed below)

STATUTE: California Code, Nonprofit Corporation Law, Public Benefit Corporations, Section 5122

Colorado

Secretary of State
Business Division
1560 Broadway, Suite 200
Denver, CO 80202-5169
303-894-2200

Website:
www.sos.state.co.us/pubs/
business/main.htm

LIMITED LIABILITY COMPANY

WHAT MUST BE FILED:

You must file the typed original and one copy of the Articles of Organization with the secretary of state. You need to include a self-addressed envelope.

ARTICLES OF ORGANIZATION SPECIAL REQUIREMENTS:

No special requirements.

STATUTES:

Colorado Limited Liability Company Act, Colorado Revised Statutes, beginning with Section 7-80-101.

CORPORATION

WHAT MUST BE FILED:

Make a copy of the fill-in-the-blanks Articles and complete both documents by typing them in black ink. File both originals and enclose the filing fee. Include a typed or machine printed self-addressed envelope.

ARTICLES REQUIREMENTS:

The minimum requirements for a Colorado nonprofit corporation are as follows:

- the corporate name
- the name and street address of the corporation's registered agent and office
- the name and address of each incorporator
- a statement whether or not the corporation will have members
- provisions regarding distribution of assets upon dissolution
- the number of directors your corporation shall have

Make sure that each incorporator listed signs the Articles.

STATUTE: Colorado Revised Statutes, Chapter 7–122 of the Colorado Nonprofit Corporation Act

Connecticut

Secretary of State
Commercial Recording Division
30 Trinity Street
Hartford, CT 06106
860-509-6002
860-509-6001

Website:
www.sots.state.ct.us/Business/
    BusinessMain.html

LIMITED LIABILITY COMPANY

WHAT MUST BE FILED:

Single copy of Articles of Organization must be filed with the secretary of state. You will receive a mailing receipt. Copies are at additional charge (see below).

ARTICLES OF ORGANIZATION SPECIAL REQUIREMENTS:

Statutory agent must sign.

STATUTES:

Connecticut Limited Liability Company Act, Pub. Act 93-267, Connecticut Statutes, Title 34.

CORPORATION

WHAT MUST BE FILED:

Type or print your Certificate of Incorporation in black ink. File only the original together with the filing fee.

ARTICLES REQUIREMENTS:

In Article 2 check the appropriate box whether your corporation shall have members and what rights they shall have. Enter the name and address of your registered agent in Article 3 and make sure the agent signs the Acceptance of appointment.

As a nonprofit, nonstock corporation the purpose of your corporation may be "to engage in any lawful act or activity for which corporations may be formed under the Connecticut Revised Non stock corporation Act" (Article 4).

STATUTE: Connecticut General Statutes, Nonstock Corporations, Sec. 33-427

Delaware

State of Delaware
Division of Corporations
John G. Townsend Building
401 Federal Street, Suite 4
Dover, DE 19901
  or (for regular mail)
P.O. Box 898
Dover, DE 19903
302-739-3073

Website:
www.state.de.us/corp

LIMITED LIABILITY COMPANY

WHAT MUST BE FILED:

The original and one copy of the Certificate of Formation must be filed with the secretary of state. The documents must be submitted in the U.S. letter size (8.5"x11") with certain margins and must be either typed, printed, or written in black ink.

ARTICLES OF ORGANIZATION SPECIAL REQUIREMENTS:

The document is called a "Certificate of Formation" in Delaware and has only three requirements, the name, address of the registered office, and name of registered agent.

STATUTES:

Title 6, Commerce and Trade, Chapter 18, Limited Liability Company Act.

CORPORATION

WHAT MUST BE FILED:

Complete the fill-in-the-blanks form Certificate of Incorporation for "nonstock corporations." Print or type your documents in black ink and submit any additional documents in the US letter size "8.5x11". File the original Certificate of Formation and one exact copy. Enclose the filing fee.

ARTICLES REQUIREMENTS:

Nonprofit corporations must add, "This Corporation shall be a nonprofit corporation" in the third Article.

In Article 4 you are asked to state your membership conditions but you can also leave that to be regulated by your Bylaws.

STATUTE: Delaware Code Annotated, Title 8, Sec. 102

District of Columbia

Department of Consumer and
    Regulatory Affairs
Corporation Division
941 North Capital Street NE
Washington, D.C. 20002
202-442-4400

Website:
http://dcra.dc.gov/dcra/site/default.asp

LIMITED LIABILITY COMPANY

WHAT MUST BE FILED:

You must file two signed originals of Articles of Organization. Attach the written consent of the registered agent.

ARTICLES OF ORGANIZATION SPECIAL REQUIREMENTS:

The registered agent must consent to his appointment.

If a general or limited partnership converts to a limited liability company, the former name and fact of conversion must be stated Articles of Organization.

STATUTES:

Title 29, Chapter 10 of the District of Columbia Code (D.C. Limited Liability Company Act of 1994).

CORPORATION

WHAT MUST BE FILED:

Draft your own Articles accordingly to the instructions and the sample Articles given by the State. Use plain bond paper, either U.S. letter or legal size. Submit two originally signed and notarized sets of Articles.

ARTICLES REQUIREMENTS:

The minimum requirements for the Articles are as follows:

- the name of the corporation
- the period of duration (this can be perpetual or a specific period)
- a specific purpose for which the corporation is organized
- a statement whether the corporation shall have members
- if your corporation shall have members, the number of classes of members and the different qualifications and rights of the members of each class
- the manner in which directors shall be elected or appointed and a statement of which class of members shall have the right to elect directors
- a provision of the regulation of the internal affairs of the corporation
- the name of the initial registered agent and the address of the initial registered office
- the number of initial directors the corporation shall have and their names and addresses
- the names and addresses of each incorporator (incorporators must be at least 21 years of age)

STATUTE: D.C. Code, Title 29, Chapter 5

Florida

Secretary of State
Division of Corporations
P.O. Box 6327
Tallahassee, FL 32314
800-755-5111

Website:
www.dos.state.fl.us/doc/index.html

LIMITED LIABILITY COMPANY

WHAT MUST BE FILED:

Unless this material has been included in your articles, one original copy of the Articles of Organization must be filed along with the Certificate of Designation of Registered Agent. An Affidavit of Membership and Contributions must also be filed unless this information is included in your articles. If you include a copy of the articles, it will be date-stamped and returned. Otherwise, you will receive an acknowledgement letter.

ARTICLES OF ORGANIZATION SPECIAL REQUIREMENTS:

If the Limited Liability Company is to be managed by one or more managers, a statement that the company is to be a manager-managed company needs to be included in the Articles.

An acceptance by the registered agent and an affidavit of membership and contributions must be either included in the Articles or on a separate form.

STATUTES:

Title 36, Chapter 608, Florida Statutes (Florida Limited Liability Company Act).

AUTHOR'S NOTE: *As this books goes to press, major revisions of the Florida Act are pending before the legislature.*

CORPORATION

WHAT MUST BE FILED:

Complete the sample Articles and file the original and one copy. Also complete the transmittal letter provided by the state and attach it to your Articles. Enclose the correct filing fee.

ARTICLES REQUIREMENTS:

The minimum requirements for the Articles are as follows:

- the name of the corporation
- the principal place of business and mailing address of the corporation
- a specific purpose for which the corporation is formed
- a statement, in which manner the directors are elected or appointed
- the name and Florida street address of your initial registered agent—make sure your registered agent signs the Articles in the space on the bottom page
- the name and signature of each incorporator

STATUTE: Florida Statutes, Chapter 617

Georgia

Secretary of State
2 Martin Luther King, Jr. Drive, S.E.
Suite 315, West Tower
Atlanta, GA 30334
404-656-2817

Website:
www.sos.state.ga.us/corporations

LIMITED LIABILITY COMPANY

WHAT MUST BE FILED:

You must file the original and one copy of the Articles of Organization and attach the Transmittal form provided by the State.

ARTICLES OF ORGANIZATION SPECIAL REQUIREMENTS:

The name of the company must be in the Articles. If the company is to be managed by someone other than the members, a clause should be added indicating who are the managers. Other information, such as the address of the company and registered agent, is to be included on the "Transmittal Information" sheet.

The Articles must be signed by all members.

STATUTES:

Title 14, Chapter 11 of the Official Code of Georgia Annotated.

CORPORATION

WHAT MUST BE FILED:

Draft your own Articles accordingly to the guidelines given by the state. Submit the original and one exact copy.   Also fill in the "Transmittal Information" form and attach it to the Articles. Enclose the filing fee.

Note that all corporations have to publish a notice of intent to incorporate in the official legal newspaper of the county in which the registered office of the corporation is located (the Clerk of Superior Court will give you advice). You must forward your notice of intent together with a $40 publication fee directly to the newspaper on the next business day after filing your Articles. A sample notice of incorporation is included in the instructions how to draft your Articles.

ARTICLES REQUIREMENTS:

The Articles must contain the following minimum:

- the name of the corporation
- a statement that the corporation is organized pursuant to the Georgia Nonprofit Corporation Code
- the name of the registered agent and the street address of its office in Georgia (a post office box address alone is not acceptable)
- the name and address of each incorporator
- a statement whether the corporation shall have members
- the mailing address of the corporation
- a signature of one of the incorporators named in the Articles

STATUTE: Georgia Code Annotated, Title 14-2-120, Sec. 2702

Hawaii

Business Registration Division
Department of Commerce
and Consumer Affairs
P.O. Box 40
Honolulu, HI 96810
808-586-2744

Website:
www.hawaii.gov/dcca

LIMITED LIABILITY COMPANY

WHAT MUST BE FILED:

You must file the original and one copy of the Articles of Organization.

ARTICLES OF ORGANIZATION SPECIAL REQUIREMENTS:

The Articles should state that the members are not liable for the debts of the company under Section 428-303(c) Hawaii Statutes.

If there are managers their names and residence addresses must be included, otherwise the name and residence addresses of the members must be listed.

STATUTES:

Title 23A, Chapter 428, Hawaii Revised Statutes.

CORPORATION

WHAT MUST BE FILED:

Complete both copies and file them with the Secretary of State. Enclose the filing fee.

ARTICLES REQUIREMENTS:

The Articles shall set forth the following minimum:

- the name of the corporation
- the address of the corporation's office
- the purpose for which the corporation is organized
- the names and street addresses of the initial directors
- the names and street addresses of the initial officer
- a statement whether the corporation shall have members
- the signature of each incorporator

STATUTE: Hawaii Revised Statutes, Title 23, Section 415B-34

Idaho

Secretary of State
Attn: Commercial Division
P.O. Box 83720
Boise, ID 83720-0080
208-334-2301

Website:
www.idsos.state.id.us/corp/corindex.htm

LIMITED LIABILITY COMPANY

WHAT MUST BE FILED:

You must file two completed originals. The fill-in-the-blank forms must be typed, if not typed or if the attachments are not included, there is an additional $20 fee for filing.

If you have questions about the correct filing, you can call the secretary of state's office at 208-334-2301.

ARTICLES OF ORGANIZATION SPECIAL REQUIREMENTS:

The address of the registered office may not be a P.O. Box, but must be a physical address in Idaho. The registered agent must sign the articles. If the management shall be vested in managers, at least one manager has to sign the Articles.

The name and address of at least one manager or member must be included.

STATUTES:

Title 53, Chapter 6, Idaho Limited Liability Company Act.

CORPORATION

WHAT MUST BE FILED:

Fill-in forms are provided by the state. File the original and one exact copy together with the filing fee.

ARTICLES REQUIREMENTS:

The Articles must contain the following minimum requirements:

- the name of the corporation
- the purpose for which the corporation is formed (this can be to transact any and all lawful activity for which a nonprofit corporation can be formed)
- the names and addresses of the initial directors
- the name of the initial registered agent and the address of the registered office
- the name and address of each incorporator
- a statement whether or not the corporation shall have members
- any other provision regarding the distribution of assets on dissolution

Make sure that each incorporator signs the Articles.

STATUTE: Idaho Statutes, Title 30, Chapter 3, *Idaho Nonprofit Corporation Act*

Illinois

Springfield Office:
  Secretary of State
  Business Services Dept.
  Michael J. Howlett Bldg.
  501 S. 2nd Street
  Room 328
  Springfield, IL 62756
  217-782-6961

Chicago Office:
  Secretary of State
  Business Services Dept.
  69 W. Washington
  Suite 1240
  Chicago, IL 60602
  312-793-3380

  Website:
  www.cyberdriveillinois.com/departments/
  business_services/home.html

LIMITED LIABILITY COMPANY

WHAT MUST BE FILED:

File the original and one copy of the signed Articles of Organization form. The form must be typed.

ARTICLES OF ORGANIZATION SPECIAL REQUIREMENTS:

If there are managers, their names and residence addresses must be included; otherwise the name and residence addresses of the members must be listed.

In Article 6 you are asked for the business purpose by (SIC) code. However, the statute states that the purpose can be "any or all lawful business."

STATUTES:

The Illinois Limited Liability Company Act, 805 ILCS 180.

CORPORATION

WHAT MUST BE FILED:

Type or print your documents in black ink and file the original and one exact copy. Enclose the filing fee.

After you receive the certificate and your file stamped Articles from the Secretary of State, you must file them with the office of the Recorder of Deeds of the county in which your registered office is located. The recording must be within 15 days after receiving your certificate.

ARTICLES REQUIREMENTS:

The purpose for which the corporation is formed (Article 4) must be a specific purpose and may not be too general or broad. A list of allowable purposes can be found in the booklet provided by the state (see page 3 of the booklet). Also in Article 4 check the appropriate box whether your corporation shall be a Condominium Association or whether your corporation shall be Cooperative Housing or Homeowner's Association.

STATUTE: Illinois Compiled Statutes Chapter 805, Act 105, 1992, *The General Not For Profit Corporation Act of 1986*

Indiana

Secretary of State
302 W. Washington, Room E018
Indianapolis, IN 46204
317-232-6576

Website:
www.in.gov/sos/business/index.html

LIMITED LIABILITY COMPANY

WHAT MUST BE FILED:

File original and two copies of the Articles of Organization with the secretary of state. Enclose the filing fee.

ARTICLES OF ORGANIZATION SPECIAL REQUIREMENTS:

No unusual clauses are required.

STATUTES:

Indiana Code Title 23, Chapter 18.

CORPORATION

WHAT MUST BE FILED:

Type or print all three copies of the fill-in-the-blanks forms and file them with the Secretary of State. Enclose the filing fee.

ARTICLES REQUIREMENTS:

In Article 3 check the appropriate box whether the corporation is a public benefit, a religious, or a mutual benefit corporation. Also check in Article 5 whether the corporation will have members. Make sure that the Articles are signed by each incorporator.

STATUTE: Indiana Code Sec. 23-17, *Indiana Nonprofit Corporation Act of 1991*

Iowa

Secretary of State
Corporations Division
Lucas Building, 1st Floor
321 East 12th Street
Des Moines, IA 50319
515-281-5204

Website:
www.sos.state.ia.us/business

LIMITED LIABILITY COMPANY

WHAT MUST BE FILED:

File only the original of your Articles of Organization. The document must be typed or printed in black ink. If all requirements are met, the Articles will be returned as filed.

ARTICLES OF ORGANIZATION SPECIAL REQUIREMENTS:

The principal office must be listed. (This may be the same as the registered office, but doesn't need to be.)

STATUTES:

Chapter 490A, Iowa Codes, Iowa Limited Liability Company Act.

CORPORATION

WHAT MUST BE FILED:

Draft your own Articles of Incorporation accordingly to the guidelines and Section 504A.29 of the Iowa Nonprofit Corporation Act. See "Articles Requirements" below for details. Deliver the original document and one exact copy together with the filing fee.

ARTICLES REQUIREMENTS:

The Articles must include the following minimum:

- the name of the corporation and the Chapter of the Code under which incorporated
- if you want your corporation to be formed for a limited time the period of duration, skip that if it shall be perpetual
- the purpose for which the organization is organized (must be a charitable, literary, educational, or scientific purpose)
- any provisions that set forth the regulation of the internal affairs of the corporation, including provisions of the distribution of assets upon dissolution
- the name of the registered agent and the address of the initial registered office
- the number and the names and addresses of the initial directors
- if applicable, any provision limiting any of the corporate powers
- the date on which the corporate existence shall begin (not more than ninety days in the future)—you can skip this, your corporation will then exist from the date the state issues the certificate of incorporation
- the name and address of each incorporator

Make sure that the person executing the documents signs and states his or her name and capacity in which he or she signs.

STATUTE: Iowa Code Sec. 504A.29

Kansas

Secretary of State
Corporation Division
Memorial Hall, 1st Floor
120 SW 10th Avenue
Topeka, KS 66612-1594
785-296-4564

Website:
www.kssos.org/business/business.html

LIMITED LIABILITY COMPANY

WHAT MUST BE FILED:

The Articles of Organization must be signed by the person forming the organization or by any member or manager. You must file the original signed copy and one duplicate, which may either be a signed or conformed copy. Enclose the filing fee.

ARTICLES OF ORGANIZATION SPECIAL REQUIREMENTS:

The address of its registered office and the address of the registered agent for service of process must be the same, but the agent can be the LLC itself.

If the members have the right to admit additional members, this must be included in the Articles along with the terms and conditions of the admission.

If the remaining members have the right to continue the business upon any event which terminates the continued membership of a member of the limited liability company, this must be included.

The names and addresses of the managers or if none, names and addresses of the members must be included.

STATUTES:

Kansas Statutes Annotated, beginning with Section 17-7601.

CORPORATION

WHAT MUST BE FILED:

Complete the fill-in-the-blanks form and file the original and one exact copy. Note that the Articles of Incorporation must be notarized. Enclose the filing fee.

ARTICLES REQUIREMENTS:

The purpose your corporation is formed for must be stated in Article 3, a general statement that the purpose is to "engage in any lawful act or activity for which nonprofit corporations may be organized under the Kansas General Corporation Code" is sufficient. You should check with the IRS prior to filing whether your purpose must be specific one.

If you want to apply for the federal tax exempt status you must check the "No" box in Article 4 to make clear that your corporation won't issue capital stock.

Enter the names and mailing addresses of the persons serving as initial directors until the first annual meeting. Make sure the incorporator (minimum of one) signs the Articles.

STATUTE: Kansas Statutes Annotated, Sec. 17-6002, Corporations

Kentucky

Commonwealth of Kentucky
Office of the Secretary of State
700 Capitol Avenue, Suite 152
Frankfort, KY 40601
502-564-3490

Website:
www.sos.state.ky.us

LIMITED LIABILITY COMPANY

WHAT MUST BE FILED:

File your typewritten (or printed) and signed Articles original accompanied by two exact copies. If the company will be managed by managers, the documents must be signed by the managers, or by a least one member. The person signing the document has to state the capacity in which she or he signs.

ARTICLES OF ORGANIZATION SPECIAL REQUIREMENTS:

The registered agent must consent to his or her appointment by signing the Articles.

STATUTES:

Chapter 275 Kentucky Statutes, Kentucky Limited Liability Company Act.

CORPORATION

WHAT MUST BE FILED:

The Articles must be typewritten or printed and signed by an incorporator if no director has been selected. File the original and two exact copies of your Articles and enclose the correct filing fee. The Secretary of State will return two "filed" stamped copies to your registered agent's office.

ARTICLES REQUIREMENTS:

The minimum requirements for the Articles are:

- the corporate name
- the purpose or purposes for which the corporation is organized
- the name of the initial registered agent and the address of its office
- the mailing address of the corporation's principal office
- the number of the initial directors and the names and mailing addresses of these persons
- the name and mailing address of each incorporator
- any provisions for distribution of assets on dissolution or final liquidation of your corporation

STATUTE: Kentucky Revised Statutes, Chapter 273

Louisiana

Secretary of State
Corporations Division
P.O. Box 94125
Baton Rouge, LA 70804-9125
225-925-4704

Website:
www.sos.louisiana.gov/comm/corp/
  corp-index.htm

LIMITED LIABILITY COMPANY

WHAT MUST BE FILED:

Complete both the Articles and the Initial Report. Both documents must be signed by the people organizing the LLC and both must be notarized. File only the originals and enclose the filing fee.

ARTICLES OF ORGANIZATION SPECIAL REQUIREMENTS:

Articles of Organization must be notarized. They must be accompanied by form 973 "Initial Report" which must be signed by all persons who signed the Articles of Organization and the registered agent and be notarized.

STATUTES:

Louisiana Revised Statutes beginning with Section 12:1301.

CORPORATION

WHAT MUST BE FILED:

To obtain a federal tax identification number call the IRS at 901-546-3920 prior to filing your Articles.

Complete the fill-in-the-blanks form provided by the state. Make sure that your registered agent signs the affidavit on the bottom of the second page. Both Articles and affidavit have to be notarized. File only the original and enclose the filing fee.

Within 30 days after filing your Articles, a multiple original or a copy certified by the Secretary of State and a copy of the Certificate of Incorporation must be filed with the office of the recorder of mortgages in the parish where the corporation's registered office is located.

ARTICLES REQUIREMENTS:

In Article 2 check the first box if you do not want the purpose of the corporation to be limited.

If you want to apply for the federal tax-exempt status you must check "Non-stock basis" in Article 9 to make clear that your corporation does not issue stock. You then have to fill in Article 10, characterizing the qualifications which must be met to be a member of your corporation.

STATUTE: Louisiana Revised Statutes, Chapter 12:203

Maine

Secretary of State
Bureau of Corporations, Elections,
    and Commissions
101 State House Station
Augusta, ME 04333-0101
207-624-7736

Website:
www.state.me.us/sos/cec/corp/corp.htm

LIMITED LIABILITY COMPANY

WHAT MUST BE FILED:

File the typewritten or printed original Articles of Organization. If the registered agent does not sign the Articles, he or she must sign the Acceptance of Appointment as Registered Agent.

ARTICLES OF ORGANIZATION SPECIAL REQUIREMENTS:

If there are managers, a statement to that effect must be included along with the minimum and maximum number of managers. If they have been selected, their names and addresses must be included.

STATUTES:

Maine Revised Statutes Title 31, Chapter 13, beginning with Section 601-762.

CORPORATION

WHAT MUST BE FILED:

Type or print your Articles in black ink. Make sure all your documents are dated by month, day and year and all bear original signatures. File the original and attach the completed Acceptance of Appoint-ment as registered agent. Make sure to enclose the correct filing fee.

ARTICLES REQUIREMENTS:

If you do not want the purpose for which your corporation is formed to be limited, just leave Article 2 blank, so that the corporation is organized for all purposes permitted under the law. Enter the number of your initial directors and of the directors to be elected on your first meeting in Article 4 and check the appropriate box in Article 5, whether or not your corporation shall have members.

Articles 6 and 7 are optional. Check with the IRS prior to filing your Articles, if your corporation has to meet the requirements stated in Article 7.

STATUTE: Maine Revisted Statutes Annotated, Title 13-B

Maryland

State Department of
  Assessments and Taxation
Corporate Charter Division
301 West Preston Street, Room 801
Baltimore, MD 21201-2395
410-767-1340
888-246-5941 (in state)

Website:
www.dat.state.md.us/sdatweb/
  sdatforms.html

LIMITED LIABILITY COMPANY

WHAT MUST BE FILED:

Type or print your Articles, handwritten documents are not accepted. Submit the signed original for filing. If you want a certified copy, add an additional $6 plus $1 to your filing check for each additional page.

ARTICLES OF ORGANIZATION SPECIAL REQUIREMENTS:

No special items are required in the Articles, but they request that the return address of the Articles be clearly noted.

STATUTES:

Maryland Code, Corps. & Ass'ns., beginning with Section 4A-101.

CORPORATION

WHAT MUST BE FILED:

Your documents must be typed. File only the original and enclose the filing fee.

ARTICLES REQUIREMENTS:

Characterize the purpose for which the corporation is formed with one or two sentences in Article 3 and make sure the purpose is charitable, religious, educational, or scientific.

Enter the minimum and maximum number of directors your corporation shall have and give the name and address of the initial director(s) in the space below.

STATUTE: Annotated Code of Maryland, Corporations and Associations, Sec. 2-104

Massachusetts

Secretary of the Commonwealth
Corporations Division
One Ashburton Place, 17th Floor
Boston, MA 02108
617-727-9640

Website:
www.sec.state.ma.us/cor

LIMITED LIABILITY COMPANY

WHAT MUST BE FILED:

File the original signed copy together with a photo-copy or a duplicate original. The documents must be signed either by the person forming the LLC, by any manager (if there are any), or by a trustee.

ARTICLES OF ORGANIZATION SPECIAL REQUIREMENTS:

If available, the Federal Employer Identification Number (FEIN) should be included on the articles. This is obtained by filing IRS form SS-4 (form 3 in appendix C). If the number is needed quickly it can be obtained over the phone (404-455-2360), but you must have form SS-4 completed and in front of you.

If there are managers, their names and residence addresses must be included. If the managers' business addresses are different from that of the LLC, their addresses must be listed.

If there is anyone other than a manager who is authorized to execute papers filed with the Corporations Division, their name and business must be included. If there are no managers, at least one member's name and business address must be listed.

STATUTES:

Annotated Laws of massachusetts, Title 22, Chapter 156C, Massachusetts Limited Liability Act.

CORPORATION

WHAT MUST BE FILED:

Complete the sample Articles and file the original document with the Secretary of State.

ARTICLES REQUIREMENTS:

The purpose your corporation is formed for can be explained in simple language in Article 2, but if you want to apply for the tax-exempt status, character-ize that purpose more specifically in Article 4. Check with the IRS for what requirements must be met to receive the tax-exemption.

STATUTE: Massachusetts General Laws, Chapter 180

Michigan

Michigan Department of Commerce
Corporation and Securities Bureau
Corporation Division
P.O. Box 30054
Lansing, MI 48909
517-241-6470

Website:
www.michigan.gov/cis

LIMITED LIABILITY COMPANY

WHAT MUST BE FILED:

The Articles must be typed or filled in with black ink. Either form C&S 700 must be used for the Articles or it should accompany your Articles.

If you prefer the fax filing procedure, fill in the "ELF Application" form (you must provide your Visa/Mastercard number here), the cover sheet, and check the fax filing checklist (provided by the State).

ARTICLES OF ORGANIZATION SPECIAL REQUIREMENTS:

The Articles of Organization must be either on form C&S 700 (which has specific spaces for filing number, date received and return address) or a "comparable document." If you have drafted your own articles, they suggest that you attach C&S 700 as a cover sheet.

STATUTES:

Act 23 of the Public Acts of 1993, Michigan Limited Liability Company Act, or Michigan Compiled Laws, beginning with Section 450.4101.

CORPORATION

WHAT MUST BE FILED:

Complete the fill-in-the-blanks form by typing or printing legibly in black ink. File only the original document together with the correct filing fee.

ARTICLES REQUIREMENTS:

Characterize the purpose for which your corporation is formed. This purpose must be specific. A general statement is not sufficient.

Complete either Article III (2) or III (3) depending on whether or not your corporation will issue stock. If you want to apply for the federal tax-exempt status your corporation will be on a non stock basis.

Note that except for educational corporations, which must have at least three incorporators, your corporation must only have one incorporator.

STATUTE: Michigan Compiled Laws, Sec. 21.197/202

Minnesota

Secretary of State
Division of Corporations
180 State Office Building
100 Reverend Dr. Martin Luther King Jr.
  Boulevard
St. Paul, MN 55155-1299
651-296-2803
877-551-6767 (greater Minnesota)

Website:
www.sos.state.mn.us

LIMITED LIABILITY COMPANY

WHAT MUST BE FILED:

Type or print your articles in black ink (illegible articles will be returned). Must have original signatures.

ARTICLES OF ORGANIZATION SPECIAL REQUIREMENTS:

Registered agent is optional. SIC code should be provided from the following list of 19 choices:

00. Agriculture, Forestry, Fishing
10. Mining
15. Construction
20. Manufacturing—Non-Durable Goods
35. Manufacturing—Durable Goods
40. Transportation
48. Communications
49. Utilities
50. Wholesale trade
54. Retail—Non-Durable Goods
57. Retail—Durable Goods
60. Finance, Insurance, Real Estate
73. Business Services
80. Health Services
83. Social Services
86. Membership Organizations
87. Engineering and Management Services
89. Other Services
90. Other

If your LLC owns, leases, or has interest in agricultural land as described in M.S. Section 500.24 this should be stated.

STATUTES:

Chapter 322 B Minnesota Statutes.

CORPORATION

WHAT MUST BE FILED:

Print or type your document(s) legibly in black ink. File only the original.

ARTICLES REQUIREMENTS:

Check the "Nonprofit Corporation" box at the top of your Articles. Enter the name of your initial registered agent and the address of its registered office in Article 2. Make sure that each incorporator (minimum of one) signs the Articles.

STATUTE: Minnesota Statutes Annotated Sec. 317A.111

Mississippi

Secretary of State
Business Services Division
P.O. Box 136
Jackson, MS 39205
601-359-1633
800-256-3494

Website:
www.sos.state.ms.us/busserv/corp/
corporations.asp

LIMITED LIABILITY COMPANY

WHAT MUST BE FILED:

For computer legibility make sure you fill in the forms exactly as described in the instructions. File the original copy signed by the person forming the limited liability company. Enclose the filing fee.

ARTICLES OF ORGANIZATION SPECIAL REQUIREMENTS:

The Mississippi form is bar coded and meant to be machine-readable. Using their form will speed up your filing, but it is not required.

You need to provide the Federal Employer Identification Number (F.E.I.N.), which must be obtained prior to filing. This is obtained by filing IRS form SS-4 (form 3 in appendix C). If the number is needed quickly it can be obtained over the phone (404-455-2360), but you must have form SS-4 completed and in front of you.

The name of the company is limited to 120 characters on the bar-coded form, and some other information is limited in the number of characters allowed.

STATUTES:

Mississippi Code beginning with Section 79-29-101.

CORPORATION

WHAT MUST BE FILED:

Complete the fill-in-the-blanks form exactly as described in the instructions. File only the original and enclose the filing fee. Attach the completed statement that your corporation is organized only for the purposes that will be recognized for the tax exemption.

ARTICLES REQUIREMENTS:

In Article 4 nonprofit corporations can determine the period of duration, enter either a certain number of years or check "perpetual."

Give the name and address of each incorporator in Article 7.

STATUTE: Mississippi Code Annotated Sec. 79-11-137

Missouri

Corporations Division
P.O. Box 778
Jefferson City, MO 65102-0778
573-751-4153
866-223-6535

Website:
www.sos.mo.gov/business/corporations/
Default.asp

LIMITED LIABILITY COMPANY

WHAT MUST BE FILED:

File the completed Articles in duplicate. Sign each copy and enclose the filing fee. If your documents conform to the filing provisions, the secretary will return the duplicate copy to the organizer.

ARTICLES OF ORGANIZATION SPECIAL REQUIREMENTS:

Missouri Statutes do not include any unusual requirements for the Articles.

STATUTES:

Chapter 347 Missouri Revised Statutes.

CORPORATION

WHAT MUST BE FILED:

Complete the fill-in-the-blanks forms and file your Articles in duplicate. Make sure both documents are originally signed. Enclose the filing fee.

ARTICLES REQUIREMENTS:

If you want to apply for the tax exempt status, make sure to meet the special requirements listed in the separate instructions. These requirements are as follows:

- the purpose for which the corporation is formed (Article 8) must be a charitable, educational, religious, or scientific one (to meet the state's requirements you also have to indicate exactly what your corporation is doing)
- the net income of the corporation may not distributed to the member, directors, or other private persons except for reasonable compensation for services rendered
- the corporation may not take part in any political or legislative activities
- upon the dissolution of the corporation the remaining assets must be distributed either for the corporation's purposes or to any other similar corporation qualified as exempt organizations

STATUTE: Missouri Revised Statutes, Chapter 347

Montana

Secretary of State
P.O. Box 202801
Helena, MT 59620-2801
406-444-3665

Website:
www.sos.state.mt.us/css/BSB/Contents.asp

LIMITED LIABILITY COMPANY

WHAT MUST BE FILED:

File the original and one copy of your signed Articles and enclose the correct filing fee.

"Priority filing" ensures twenty-four hour turn-around for an additional fee.

ARTICLES OF ORGANIZATION SPECIAL REQUIREMENTS:

The registered agent must sign the Articles. If there are managers, their names and residence addresses must be included; otherwise, the name and residence addresses of the members must be listed.

STATUTES:

Title 35, Chapter 8, Montana Code Annotated.

CORPORATION

WHAT MUST BE FILED:

First you have to check if the chosen name of your corporation is available. For this information you have to call the office of the Secretary of State. Then file the fill-in-the-blanks Articles and make a copy of the completed Articles. Mail both documents to the Secretary of State and enclose the filing fee.

ARTICLES REQUIREMENTS:

Your Articles have to include at least the following contents:

- corporate name
- name and address of the registered agent and office in Montana
- name and address of each incorporator
- the specific purpose of the corporation (because the Internal Revenue Service requires specific language in order to qualify for nonprofit tax status it is advised that you contact the IRS)
- a statement whether the corporation will have members
- distribution of assets in the case of dissolution

STATUTE: Montana Revised Statutes Sec. 35-2-202

Nebraska

Corporations Division
P.O. Box 94608
Lincoln, NE 68509-4608
402-471-4079

Website:
www.sos.state.ne.us/business/corp_serv

LIMITED LIABILITY COMPANY

WHAT MUST BE FILED:

Two copies of the Articles.

ARTICLES OF ORGANIZATION SPECIAL
REQUIREMENTS:

Must include the cash and property contributed as
stated capital and events which will trigger the con-
tribution of additional capital, if any. All managers'
names and addresses, or if managed by members, all
members' names and addresses must be listed.

Duration cannot exceed thirty years.

STATUTES:

Chapter 21, beginning with Section 2601 Nebraska
Limited Liability Company Act.

CORPORATION

WHAT MUST BE FILED:

You have to draw your own Articles. Follow the
instructions given by the state. The document must
be executed by an incorporator. The executing
incorporator has to state her or his name and capacity ("incorporator") beneath or opposite the signature. Send the original and one copy to the secretary
of state for filing. Make sure that you enclose the
correct filing fee.

ARTICLES REQUIREMENTS:

Articles have to include the following basic contents:

- the corporate name
- a statement about the general purpose of the
  corporation (public benefit corporation,
  mutual-benefit corporation or religious corporation)
- street address (post office box is not acceptable) of corporation's registered office and
  the name of its initial registered agent at that
  office
- name and street address of each incorporator
- a statement whether or not the corporation
  will have members
- provisions not consistent with the law
  regarding the distribution of assets on dissolution

STATUTE: Nebraska Revised Statutes Chapter 21-
1905 et seq.

Nevada

Secretary of State
202 North Carson Street
Carson City, NV 89701-4201
775-684-5708

Website:
www.sos.state.nv.us

LIMITED LIABILITY COMPANY

WHAT MUST BE FILED:

File the original and as many copies of it as you want certified and returned to you. The articles must be acknowledged by a notary. Enclose the filing fee with an additional $20 for each certification.

ARTICLES OF ORGANIZATION SPECIAL REQUIREMENTS:

If the company is to be managed by managers, their names and addresses must be included, otherwise the names and addresses of the members must be included.

STATUTES:

Chapter 86 Nevada Revised Statutes.

CORPORATION

WHAT MUST BE FILED:

Type or print your Articles in black ink only. File the original and as many copies as you want to be certified and returned to you. Note that you must at least keep one certified copy in the office of your resident agent. Make sure that each incorporator's signature is notarized.

ARTICLES REQUIREMENTS:

Enter the name and address of the initial resident agent in Article 2 and make sure that agent signs the certificate of acceptance on the bottom of the page.

To characterize the purpose for which the corporation is formed in accordance to the IRS requirements check with the IRS prior to filing.

Give the names and addresses of the initial Governing Board in Article 4. Do not forget that each incorporator's signature must be notarized.

STATUTE: Nevada Revised Statutes Chapter 82

New Hampshire

Corporation Division Department of State
107 North Main Street
Concord, NH 03301-4989
603-271-3244

Website:
www.sos.nh.gov/corporate

LIMITED LIABILITY COMPANY

WHAT MUST BE FILED:

The Certificate of Formation must be filed in duplicate and signed by a member or manager with his or her capacity designated. It must be accompanied by form LCC 1-A, Addendum to Certificate of Formation.

ARTICLES OF ORGANIZATION SPECIAL REQUIREMENTS:

The Certificate of Formation must list the nature of the primary business, but you may add the authority "to perform any lawful business permitted for limited liability companies under the state law." In New Hampshire, your LLC must certify in a separate addendum (Form LLC 1-A) that it meets the requirements of the New Hampshire Securities Law. If the aggregate number of holders of the company's securities does not exceed ten, provides that no advertising has been published in connection with any security sale, and all securities sales are consummated within sixty days after the date of the formation of the company, then the company is exempt from securities registration. If your company meets these requirements, check line 1 in the Addendum. If your company has or will register its securities for sale in New Hampshire, enter the date the registration statement was or will be filed with the Bureau of Securities Regulation in line 2. If you can take advantage of another exemption from the registration requirement, cite this exemption in line 3.

STATUTES:

New Hampshire Revised Statutes Annotated, beginning with Section 304-C:1.

CORPORATION

WHAT MUST BE FILED:

Print or type your documents in black ink and leave one-inch margins on both sides.

File the original and one exact copy. Both documents must bear original signatures. Note that your Articles of Agreement must be filed with the clerk of the city or town of the principal place of business prior to filing with the Secretary of State. Enclose the filing fee.

ARTICLES REQUIREMENTS:

The most important requirement for forming your nonprofit corporation is that you need five or more incorporators.

The legal purposes your corporation may be formed for are listed in Chapter 292:1 of the New Hampshire Revised Statutes.

In Article 7 you have the opportunity to make provisions eliminating or limiting the personal liability of a director or officer of your corporation.

STATUTE: New Hampshire Revised Statutes Annotated Chapter 292

New Jersey

New Jersey Division of Revenue
Corporate Filing Unit
P.O. Box 628
Trenton, NJ 08646-0628
609-292-9292

Website:
www.state.nj.us/njbgs/index.html

LIMITED LIABILITY COMPANY

WHAT MUST BE FILED:

You need to file the "Public Records Filing for New Business Entity" form and the "Business Registration" form. Those forms are for any new business, so make sure to check that you are forming a limited liability company.

To take part in the fax-filing program which offers same or next day filing, complete the "Facsimile Filing Service Request" and fax this request together with your completed Certificate of Formation to 609-984-6851. Payment method for this program is either by Visa/MC or Discover, or you have to give your depository account number. Note that there is an extra filing fee for the fax service (see "Filing Fees").

ARTICLES OF ORGANIZATION SPECIAL REQUIREMENTS:

You need to put in a type code in No. 2. The type code for your limited liability company is "LLC" (for a foreign: "FLC").

STATUTES:

New Jersey Revised Statutes Title 42:2B.

CORPORATION

WHAT MUST BE FILED:

Type your documents in black ink. File the original and two exact copies. Enclose a self-addressed stamped envelope to receive a filed copy and the correct filing fee.

ARTICLES REQUIREMENTS:

To obtain the tax exempt status after filing your Articles make sure the purpose for which your corporation is organized (Article 2) will meet the IRS requirements for tax exemption.

You can leave most of the regulation for the corporations inner affairs to your bylaws if you do not want these affairs to be regulated by the Certificate of Incorporation.

STATUTE: New Jersey Statutes Sec. 15A:2-8

New Mexico

Public Regulation Commission
P.O. Box 1269
Santa Fe, NM 87504-1269
505-827-4502
505-827-4508
800-947-4722
(New Mexico residents only)

Website:
www.nmprc.state.nm.us/corporations/
corpshome.htm

LIMITED LIABILITY COMPANY

WHAT MUST BE FILED:

An original and duplicate of Articles of Organization together with the notarized affidavit of the person appointed as your registered agent. Enclose the appropriate filing fee.

The filing office also accepts faxed filing documents.

ARTICLES OF ORGANIZATION SPECIAL REQUIREMENTS:

A notarized affidavit accepting appointment must be provided by the registered agent.

STATUTES:

New Mexico Statutes Annotated Title 53, Chapter 19.

CORPORATION

WHAT MUST BE FILED:

Type or print your Articles legibly in black ink. File duplicate originals and attach the completed, signed and notarized affidavit of acceptance of your registered agent. Enclose the correct filing fee.

ARTICLES REQUIREMENTS:

The minimum requirements for forming the corporation are as follows:

- the name of the corporation
- the period of its duration, which may be perpetual
- a definition of the purpose for which the corporation is formed
- provisions regulating the internal affairs of the corporation including provisions for distributing remaining assets upon the dissolution of the corporation
- the name of its initial agent and the address of the agent's office
- the number of persons serving as the initial directors and the names and addresses of these directors
- the name and address of each incorporator

STATUTE: New Mexico Statutes Annotated Chapter 53-8-31

New York

NYS Department of State
Division of Corporations
41 State Street
Albany, N.Y. 12231-0001
518-473-2492

Website:
www.dos.state.ny.us/corp/corpwww.html

LIMITED LIABILITY COMPANY

WHAT MUST BE FILED:

An original and duplicate of Articles of Organization.

If you reserved a name prior to filing, enclose a copy of the certificate of name registration.

ARTICLES OF ORGANIZATION SPECIAL REQUIREMENTS:

The secretary of state should be designated as agent for service of process. The county of the principal office must be listed.

Notice of formation must be published in two publications of general circulation, once a week for six weeks.

STATUTES:

Chapter 34 of the Consolidated Law, New York Limited Liability Company Law.

CORPORATION

WHAT MUST BE FILED:

If you draft your own Articles of Incorporation (not using the forms) make sure that your documents contain a separate page which sets forth the title of the document being submitted and the name and address of the person to which the receipt for filing shall be mailed. Enclose the filing fee.

ARTICLES REQUIREMENTS:

The Certificate of Incorporation must set forth the following minimum:

- the name of the corporation
- a statement that the corporation is formed pursuant to subparagraph (a)(5) of Section 102 of the Not-For-Profit Corporation Law, the type of corporation it shall be under section 201 (Type A-D), and the purpose for which the corporation is formed
- the county where the corporate office is to be located
- the name and address of each director, if your corporation is an A, B, or C type corporation
- the duration of the corporation, if not perpetual
- a designation of the Secretary of State as agent of the corporation upon whom process may be served and the P.O. address to which the secretary of state shall mail a copy on any process against it served upon him or her
- if applicable, the name of the registered agent and the address of its initial registered office and a statement that he or she is the agent upon whom process against the corporation may be served
- any provision for the regulation of the internal affairs of the corporation that is not inconsistent with the law (e.g., types or classes of membership, distribution of assets upon dissolution, etc.)

STATUTE: New York Not-For-Profit Corporation Law, Sec. 402

North Carolina

Corporations Division
P.O. Box 29622
Raleigh, NC 27626-0622
919-807-2225

Website:
www.secretary.state.nc.us./corporations

LIMITED LIABILITY COMPANY

WHAT MUST BE FILED:

An original and duplicate of Articles of Organization.

ARTICLES OF ORGANIZATION SPECIAL REQUIREMENTS:

Name and address of each organizer is required.

STATUTES:

North Carolina General Statutes Title 57C.

CORPORATION

WHAT MUST BE FILED:

Draft your Articles accordingly to the sample and the instructions given in the booklet. File the original and one exact copy together with the filing fee.

After filing the copy will be returned "file-stamped" to the incorporator(s).

ARTICLES REQUIREMENTS:

The Articles of Incorporation require the following minimum:

- the corporate name
- a statement, whether the corporation shall be a "charitable or religious corporation" pursuant to the North Carolina. General Statutes Sec. 55A-2-02 (a)(2)
- the name of the initial registered agent and the street address of its initial registered office (if mailing address is different, give the mailing address)
- the name and address of each incorporator (at least one incorporator required)
- a statement whether the corporation shall have members
- provisions regarding the distribution of assets upon the dissolution of the corporation
- the street address (and, if different, the mailing address) and county of the principal office
- the signature and capacity of each incorporator

STATUTE: North Carolina General Statutes, Chapter 55A

North Dakota

Secretary of State
600 East Boulevard Avenue
Department 108
Bismarck, ND 58505-0500
701-328-4284
or 800-352-0867 ext. 8-4284

Website:
www.state.nd.us/sec/businessserv

LIMITED LIABILITY COMPANY

WHAT MUST BE FILED:

An original and duplicate of Articles of Organization and a Registered Agent Consent to Serve.

ARTICLES OF ORGANIZATION SPECIAL REQUIREMENTS:

Must include name and address of each organizer.

STATUTES:

North Dakota Century Code. Chapter 10-32.

CORPORATION

WHAT MUST BE FILED:

Complete the Articles and file in duplicate. Attach the signed consent to serve and enclose the filing fee for the Articles and for the consent.

ARTICLES REQUIREMENTS:

The Articles require the following minimum:

- the name of the corporation
- if not perpetual, the duration of its existence
- a specific characterization of the purpose for which the corporation is formed
- provisions for the distribution of assets upon the dissolution or final liquidation of the corporation
- the name of the initial registered agent and the address of the agent's registered office
- the number of your initial directors and their names and addresses

STATUTE: North Dakota Century Code Chapter 10-33

Ohio

Secretary of State
Corporations Division
180 East Broad Street
Columbus, OH 43215
614-466-3910
877-767-3453

Website:
www.sos.state.oh.us/sos/
   busiserv/index.html

LIMITED LIABILITY COMPANY

WHAT MUST BE FILED:

One copy of each of Articles of Organization and Original Appointment of Agent. The Appointment must be signed by a majority of members and by the agent.

ARTICLES OF ORGANIZATION SPECIAL REQUIREMENTS:

The Articles must be accompanied by an Original Appointment of Agent signed by a majority of members and by the agent.

STATUTES:

Title 17, Chapter 1705 of the Ohio Revised Code, Limited Liability Companies.

CORPORATION

WHAT MUST BE FILED:

Complete the fill-in-the-blanks Articles and file them with the Secretary of State. Make sure that the Articles are signed by the incorporators and their names are printed or typed beneath their signatures. Enclose the filing fee. The trustees do not have to sign the Articles.

ARTICLES REQUIREMENTS:

The basic requirements are as follows:

- the corporate name
- the names and addresses of the initial trustees (not fewer than three natural persons)
- name and address of a statutory agent
- the specific purpose of the corporation (a general purpose clause will not be accepted)

STATUTE: Ohio Revised Code, Chapter 1702.04

Oklahoma

Secretary of State
Business Filing Department
2300 North Lincoln Boulevard
Room 101
101 State Capitol Building
Oklahoma City, OK 73105-4897
405-521-3912

Website:
www.sos.state.ok.us/business/
    business_filing.htm

LIMITED LIABILITY COMPANY

WHAT MUST BE FILED:

Two copies of the Articles must be filed.

ARTICLES OF ORGANIZATION SPECIAL
REQUIREMENTS:

No unusual requirements.

STATUTES:

Title 18, Chapter 32 of the Oklahoma Statutes,
Oklahoma Limited Liability Company Act.

CORPORATION

WHAT MUST BE FILED:

Type or print your documents clearly and file the
original in duplicate. Enclose the filing fee.

ARTICLES REQUIREMENTS:

The basic requirements are as follows:

- the corporate name
- the name of the initial registered agent and
  the address of its initial registered office
- if the corporation is a church, the street
  address of its location
- if not perpetual, the duration of your corporation
- the specific purpose for which the corporation is formed
- the number, names, and mailing addresses of
  the initial directors
- the names and mailing address of each incorporator

Make sure that each incorporator signs the Articles.

STATUTE: Oklahoma Statutes, Title 18, *Oklahoma
General Corporation Act*

Oregon

State of Oregon
Corporation Division
255 Capitol Street NE
Suite 151
Salem, OR 97310-1327
503-986-2200
Fax: 503-378-4381

Website:
www.filinginoregon.com

LIMITED LIABILITY COMPANY

WHAT MUST BE FILED:

Original and one copy.

ARTICLES OF ORGANIZATION SPECIAL
REQUIREMENTS:

Name and address of each organizer must be
included.

STATUTES:

Title 7, Chapter 63 Oregon Revised Statutes, Oregon
Limited Liability Company Act.

CORPORATION

WHAT MUST BE FILED:

Type or print the Articles in black ink. If you file
your documents by mail, attach one exact copy of
the original. Enclose the filing fee.

ARTICLES REQUIREMENTS:

The basic requirements are as follows:

- corporate name
- name and address of registered agent (the
  address must be an Oregon street address and
  identical with the agent's business office, post
  office boxes are not acceptable)
- additional the agent's mailing address
- corporation's address for mailing notices
- type of corporation (public benefit, mutual
  benefit, religious)
- a statement whether the corporation will
  have members or not
- a statement concerning the distribution of
  assets upon dissolution
- names and addresses of all incorporators

Make sure that each incorporator signs the document and print or typewrite the names beneath the
signatures.

STATUTE: Oregon Revised Statutes, Chapter 65
Oregon Business Corporation Act

Pennsylvania

Department of State
Corporation Bureau
206 North Office Building
Harrisburg, PA 17120
717-787-1057

Website:
www.dos.state.pa.us/corps/site/default.asp

LIMITED LIABILITY COMPANY

WHAT MUST BE FILED:

One original Certificate of Organization– Domestic Limited Liability Company and one copy of the completed docketing statement (form DSCB:15-134A).

Also include either a self-addressed, stamped postcard with the filing information noted or a self-addressed, stamped envelope with a copy of the filing document to receive confirmation of the file date prior to receiving the microfilmed original.

ARTICLES OF ORGANIZATION SPECIAL REQUIREMENTS:

Must list names and addresses of all members and organizers.

STATUTES:

Title 15, Chapter 89, Pennsylvania Consolidated Statutes.

CORPORATION

WHAT MUST BE FILED:

Print or type your documents in black or blue-black ink. File the original of your Articles of Incorporation, attach a cover letter and enclose the following:

- one copy of the completed docketing statement (form DSCB: 15-134A)—this form is provided by the state
- if applicable, copies of the Consent to Appropri-ation of Name or, copies of the Consent to Use of Similar Name
- the filing fee

Also include either a self-addressed, stamped postcard with the filing information noted or a self-addressed, stamped envelope with a copy of the filing document to receive confirmation of the file date prior to receiving the microfilmed original.

ARTICLES REQUIREMENTS:

If you want to apply for the federal tax exemption, check with the IRS prior to filing your Articles to make sure your corporation meets the special purpose required to qualify for the tax exemption (purpose must be given in Article 3).

Give the name and address of each incorporator in Article 8 (minimum of one incorporator).

STATUTE: Pennsylvania Consolidated Statutes Title 15

Rhode Island

Secretary of State
Corporations Division
100 North Main Street
Providence, RI 02903
401-222-3040

Website:
www.sec.state.ri.us/us/corps

LIMITED LIABILITY COMPANY

WHAT MUST BE FILED:

Two signed copies of the Articles of Organization must be filed.

ARTICLES OF ORGANIZATION SPECIAL REQUIREMENTS:

A statement should be included indicating whether the company is to be taxed as a corporation or pass-through entity.

STATUTES:

Title 7, Chapter 16 of the General Laws of Rhode Island.

CORPORATION

WHAT MUST BE FILED:

Complete and sign the original and the duplicate Articles. Enclose the filing fee.

When the Articles are properly completed, a Certificate of Incorporation, together with the file stamped original will be returned to you.

ARTICLES REQUIREMENTS:

The minimum requirements are as follows:

- the corporate name
- if not perpetual, the duration of the corporation
- the specific purpose your corporation is formed for (if you want to apply for the federal tax exemption, check with the IRS prior to filing if your corporation must meet specific requirements)
- any provisions for regulating the corporation's internal affairs
- the name of the initial registered agent and the address of its initial registered office
- the number of directors and their names and addresses
- the name and address of each incorporator

Make sure that each incorporator signs the Articles.

STATUTE: General Laws Rhode Island Chapter 7-6-34

South Carolina

Secretary of State
P.O. Box 11350
Columbia, SC 29211
803-734-2158

Website:
www.scsos.com/corporations.htm

LIMITED LIABILITY COMPANY

WHAT MUST BE FILED:

File the completed original and one copy (duplicate, original, or conformed copy). Enclose the filing fee.

ARTICLES OF ORGANIZATION SPECIAL REQUIREMENTS:

On the Articles of Organization form provided by the state, article 7 allows the company to designate one or more of its members to be liable for company debts. This is neither required nor recommended and defeats the purpose of the limited liability company.

STATUTES:

Chapter 33-44 of the South Carolina Code of 1976.

CORPORATION

WHAT MUST BE FILED:

File the completed original and either a duplicate original or a conformed copy. Enclose the filing fee.

ARTICLES REQUIREMENTS:

In Article 3 check the appropriate box whether the corporation is a public benefit, religious, or mutual benefit corporation. If you want to apply for the federal tax exemption and your corporation is either a public benefit or religious corporation, check the "a" box in Article 6 to make sure that upon dissolution of the corporation, the assets will be distributed accordingly to the tax exempt purposes. If you form a mutual benefit corporation check one of the two dissolution statements in Article 7.

Each incorporator (minimum of one) must sign the Articles.

STATUTE: South Carolina Code Annotated Chapter 33-44

South Dakota

Secretary of State
Capitol Building
500 East Capital Avenue
Suite 204
Pierre, SD 57501
605-773-4845

Website:
www.sdsos.gov/corporations

LIMITED LIABILITY COMPANY

WHAT MUST BE FILED:

Two copies of the Articles of Organization and a First Annual Report.

ARTICLES OF ORGANIZATION SPECIAL REQUIREMENTS:

The duration of the LLC can be for no more than thirty years (though it can be extended in the future). Total cash, property, and services contributed must be listed as well as requirements for future contributions.

If there are managers, their names and residence addresses must be included; otherwise, the name and residence addresses of the members must be listed.

On the Articles of Organization form provided by the state, Article 7 allows the company to designate one or more of its members to be liable for company debts. This is neither required nor recommended and defeats the purpose of the limited liability company.

A first Annual Report must be filed along with the Articles.

STATUTES:

South Dakota Codified Laws, Title 47, Chapters 34 and 34A.

CORPORATION

WHAT MUST BE FILED:

Type the Articles and file the original document and one exact copy. Make sure that the consent of appointment is signed by the registered agent and that the Articles are notarized. Enclose the filing fee.

ARTICLES REQUIREMENTS:

The Articles must contain the following minimum:

- the name of the corporation
- if not perpetual, the period of existence
- the purpose for which the corporation is formed—this clause must contain sufficient information to determine the type of purpose (types of purposes are given in Section 47-22-4 of the statutes)
- a statement whether the corporation shall have members and if so, provisions regulating the class of members and their rights
- regulations concerning the method of election of the directors
- any provisions regulating the internal affairs of the corporation
- the street address of your initial registered office and the name or your initial registered agent
- the number of directors and their names and addresses
- the names and addresses of the incorporators (minimum of three)
- the signature of each incorporator

STATUTE: South Dakota Codified Laws Chapter 47

Tennessee

Department of State
Corporate Filings
312 Eighth Avenue North
6th Floor
William R. Snodgrass Tower
Nashville, TN 37243
615-741-2286

Website:
www.tennessee.gov/sos/bus_svc/index.htm

LIMITED LIABILITY COMPANY

WHAT MUST BE FILED:

Only one original Articles of Organization must be filed.

ARTICLES OF ORGANIZATION SPECIAL REQUIREMENTS:

The name and address of each organizer must be listed. The county and zip code of the registered office and the principle executive office must be included with their addresses. The number of members must be listed.

If a member can be expelled and if there are prescriptive rights, these must be spelled out in the Articles. It is possible to designate one or more of its members to be liable for company debts. This is neither required nor recommended, as it defeats the purpose of the limited liability company.

STATUTES:

Tennessee Code Annotated, Sections 48-201-101 through 48-248-606.

CORPORATION

WHAT MUST BE FILED:

Type or print the Articles in black ink using either the fill-in-the-blanks form or, if drafting your own documents, using legal or letter size paper. The documents must be executed either by an incorporator, by the chair of the board of directors, or by a trustee. File only the original document(s) together with the filing fee.

ARTICLES REQUIREMENTS:

The charter must contain the following minimum:

- the corporate name
- a statement whether the corporation is a public or mutual benefit corporation or whether it is a religious corporation
- the address of the initial registered office and the name of the initial registered agent
- the name and address of each incorporator
- the street address of the principal office (may be the same as the address of the registered agent)
- a statement that the corporation is not for profit
- a statement that there will be no members
- provisions regarding the distribution of assets upon the dissolution of the corporation

STATUTE: Tennessee Code Annotated Section 48-52

Texas

Corporations Section
Office of the Secretary of State
P.O. Box 13697
Austin, TX 78711
512-463-5555

Website:
www.sos.state.tx.us/corp/index.shtml

LIMITED LIABILITY COMPANY

WHAT MUST BE FILED:

Two copies of the Articles must be filed. Use the P. O. Box for mail. For courier use: James Earl Rudder, Office Building, 1019 Brazos, Austin, TX 78701.

ARTICLES OF ORGANIZATION SPECIAL REQUIREMENTS:

The name and address of each organizer must be included.

STATUTES:

Texas Rev. Civil Statutes Annotated Art. 1528n, Texas Limited Liability Company Act.

CORPORATION

WHAT MUST BE FILED:

Draft your own Articles accordingly to the instructions provided by the state or fill out the form provided. File two copies of these together with the filing fee. The filing office will return one filed stamped copy.

ARTICLES REQUIREMENTS:

The minimum contents of your Articles are as follows:

- the name of the corporation
- the period of duration, which may be perpetual
- a statement that the corporation is not for profit
- the specific purpose for which the corporation is formed (check with the IRS prior to filing what requirements your corporation has to meet to qualify for the federal tax exemption)
- the name of the registered agent and the address of the registered office.
- a statement whether the corporation shall have members
- if the management of the corporation shall be vested in the members, a statement to that effect
- the number of the initial board of directors and the names and addresses of your directors
- the name and street address of each incorporator
- provisions regarding the distribution of assets upon the dissolution of the corporation

Make sure that each incorporator signs the Articles.

STATUTE: Texas Nonprofit Corporation Act, Article 1396-3.02

Utah

Department of Commerce
Division of Corporations and
   Commercial Code
P.O. Box 146705
Salt Lake City, UT 84114-6705
801-530-4849
877-526-3994 (in state)

Website:
www.commerce.utah.gov/cor/index.html

LIMITED LIABILITY COMPANY

WHAT MUST BE FILED:

File one original and one exact copy of your
Articles. You can deliver the documents personally,
by mail or by fax. If you choose to fax your documents, make sure to include the number of your
Visa/MasterCard and the expiration date.

ARTICLES OF ORGANIZATION SPECIAL
REQUIREMENTS:

The period of duration cannot exceed ninety-nine
years. If there are managers, their names and residence addresses must be included, otherwise the
name and residence addresses of the members must
be listed.

STATUTES:

Utah Code Annotated, Title 48-2B.

CORPORATION

WHAT MUST BE FILED:

File one original and one exact copy of your self-
drafted Articles. At least one document must bear
the original signature. You can deliver the documents personally, by mail, or even by fax. If you
choose to fax your documents, make sure to include
the number of your Visa/Mastercard and the expiration date.

ARTICLES REQUIREMENTS:

The minimum of what the Articles must contain is:

- the corporate name
- the term of the corporation's existence
- the purpose or purposes for which your
  corporation is formed—this must include
  the statement that it is organized as a nonprofit corporation
- the address of the corporation's principal
  office
- a statement whether or not the corporation
  shall have members
- the number of initial trustees your corporation shall have and their names and addresses
- the name and street address of each incorporator (at least one)
- the name of the corporation's initial registered agent and the street address of the registered office
- the signature of each incorporator

The Articles also must include a statement by your
registered agent that he or she acknowledges his or
her acceptance as registered agent.

STATUTE: Utah Code Annotated, Section 16-6-46
Corporation Laws

Vermont

Secretary of State
81 River Street
Montpelier, VT 05609-1104
802-828-2386

Website:
www.sec.state.vt.us/corps/corpindex.htm

LIMITED LIABILITY COMPANY

WHAT MUST BE FILED:

The original and one exact copy.

ARTICLES OF ORGANIZATION SPECIAL
REQUIREMENTS:

The name and address of each organizer are
required.

It is possible to designate one or more of the company's members to be liable for company debts. This
is neither required nor recommended, as it defeats
the purpose of the limited liability company.
However, you need to include a statement about it
in your Articles.

STATUTES:

Vermont Statutes Annotated, Title 11, Chapter 21,
beginning with Section 3001.

CORPORATION

WHAT MUST BE FILED:

Complete the fill-in-the-blanks form by typewriting
or printing. File the original and one exact copy.
Enclose the filing fee.

ARTICLES REQUIREMENTS:

The minimum requirements are as follows:

- the corporate name
- the name of the registered agent
- the street address of the registered office
- if not perpetual, the period of duration
- a statement, whether the corporation shall be
  a public benefit, mutual benefit, nonprofit
  corporation, or a cooperative
- the names and addresses of your initial directors
- if applicable, the names and addresses of
  your members
- the specific purpose for which your corporation is formed
- provisions regarding the distribution of
  assets upon the dissolution of the corporation
- signatures and addresses of each incorporator

STATUTE: Vermont Statutes Annotated, Title 11,
Nonprofit Corporations

Virginia

Clerk of the State
  Corporation Commission
P.O. Box 1197
Richmond, VA 23218
804-371-9733

Website:
www.state.va.us/scc/division/clk

LIMITED LIABILITY COMPANY

WHAT MUST BE FILED:

The Articles must be printed or typewritten in black ink. Complete and file the original form and enclose the filing fee.

ARTICLES OF ORGANIZATION SPECIAL REQUIREMENTS:

The registered agent must be an individual who is a Virginia resident and either a member or an officer, director or partner of a member of the LLC, or a Virginia State Bar member, or an organization registered under Va. Code Section 54.1-3902 (an attorney's PC, PLLC, or PRLLP) and this must be stated in the Articles.

The city or county of the registered agent must be included and also the post office address of the office where the records will be kept.

The Articles can be executed by any person.

STATUTES:

Title 13.1 of the Code of Virginia.

CORPORATION

WHAT MUST BE FILED:

For forming a nonprofit corporation take form SCC 819 (nonstock corporation). Type or write your Articles in black ink. Complete and file only the original form and enclose the filing fee.

ARTICLES REQUIREMENTS:

The minimum requirements for filing the Articles are as follows:

- the corporate name
- a statement whether or not your corporation shall have members and if so, provisions designating the classes of members and their rights
- a statement of the manner in which directors shall be elected or appointed
- the name of the initial registered agent and its status
- the address of your registered office
- optional provisions regarding the purpose for which the corporation is formed (to meet the special requirements for obtaining the federal tax exempt status, check with the IRS prior to filing the Articles for which requirements have to be met)
- if the corporation shall have initial directors, state the number of directors and their names and addresses
- the signature and printed name of each incorporator

STATUTE: Virginia Code Annotated Title 13.1 Chapter 10

Washington

Secretary of State
Corporations Division
P.O. Box 40234
Olympia, WA 98504-0234
360-753-7115

Website:
www.secstate.wa.gov/corps

LIMITED LIABILITY COMPANY

WHAT MUST BE FILED:

Type or print the document in black ink. Submit original and one copy. If expedited service is desired write "expedited" in bold letters on outside of envelope and include the additional fee.

ARTICLES OF ORGANIZATION SPECIAL REQUIREMENTS:

There are no unusual requirements.

STATUTES:

Chapter 25.15 Revised Code of Washington.

CORPORATION

WHAT MUST BE FILED:

Type or print the document in black ink. Submit the original and one copy together with the filing fee.

An expedited service (filing within 24 hours) is available for an extra $20 fee. If you want the expedited service write "expedited" in bold letters on outside of envelope.

ARTICLES REQUIREMENTS:

At a minimum, the Articles must contain the following:

- the name of the corporation
- if wanted, a specific effective date of incorporation
- the term of existence
- the purpose for which the corporation is formed
- provisions regulating the distribution of assets upon dissolution of the corporation
- the name and street address of the initial registered agent and a signature by this agent, acknowledging acceptance
- the name and address of each initial director
- the name and address of each incorporator
- the signature of each incorporator

STATUTE: Washington Revised Code Chapter 24.03

West Virginia

Secretary of State
Building 1, Suite 157-K
1900 Kanawha Boulevard East
Charleston, WV 25305-0770
304-558-8000

Website:
www.wvsos.com/business/main.htm

LIMITED LIABILITY COMPANY

WHAT MUST BE FILED:

Two original copies of the Articles of Organization must be filed.

ARTICLES OF ORGANIZATION SPECIAL REQUIREMENTS:

It is possible to designate members to be liable for company debts. This is neither required nor recommended, as it defeats the purpose of the limited liability company. However, the statement needs to be included in your Articles.

STATUTES:

Chapter 31B, beginning with Section 1-101, Uniform Limited Liability Company Act.

CORPORATION

WHAT MUST BE FILED:

Complete the Articles and file both originals. Make sure that the incorporator(s) file both documents and that the documents are notarized. Enclose the filing fee.

ARTICLES REQUIREMENTS:

The fill-in-the-blanks form provided by the State is both for stock and non-stock (nonprofit) corporations. Check the "nonprofit" box in Article 5 to denote your corporation structure. Then state the purpose your corporation is formed for in Article 7 and check the appropriate box whether provisions regulating the internal affairs of the corporation shall be set forth in the bylaws or are attached to the Articles. Give the names and street addresses of the incorporators in Article 10 and the names and number of initial directors in Article 11.

Name at least one person who shall have signature authority on documents filed with the Secretary of State (annual report). The incorporators must sign the Articles. Make sure that the signatures are notarized.

STATUTE: West Virginia Code Section 31-1-27

Wisconsin

Department of Financial Institutions
Division of Corporate and
　Consumer Services
P.O. Box 7846
Madison, WI 53707-7846
608-261-7577

Website:
www.wisconsin.gov or
www.wdfi.org/corporations

LIMITED LIABILITY COMPANY

WHAT MUST BE FILED:

Original and one copy must be filed.

For expedited service (filing procedure will be complete the next business day), mark your documents "For Expedited Service" and provide an extra $25 for each item. Indicate on the back side of your Articles where you would like the acknowledgement copy of the filed document sent.

Use the above address for mail. For courier delivery use 345 West Washington Avenue, 3rd Floor, Madison, WI 53703.

ARTICLES SPECIAL OF ORGANIZATION REQUIREMENTS:

The Articles for a Wisconsin LLC can only contain items of information such as:

- The name
- The street address of the initial registered office
- The name of the initial registered agent at the above address
- Whether management is vested in the members or manager(s)
- The name, address, and signature of each organizer
- A statement that the company is organized under Wisconsin statutes, Chapter 183
- The name of the person who drafted the articles

Other terms between members can be included in the operating agreement.

STATUTES:

Chapter 183 of the Wisconsin Statutes.

CORPORATION

WHAT MUST BE FILED:

Complete the fill-in-the-blanks forms and send the original and one copy to the Department of Financial Institutions. Enclose the filing fee. For expedited service (filing procedure will be completed the next business day), mark your documents "For Expedited Service" and provide an extra $25 for each item. Indicate on the back side of your Articles where the acknowledgement copy of the filed document should be sent.

ARTICLES REQUIREMENTS:

The minimum requirements are as follows:

- corporate name
- the phrase: "The corporation is organized under Chapter 181 of the Wisconsin Statutes"
- name and address of the registered agent (street address of the agent's office is required, post office box address may be part of the address, but is sufficient alone)
- mailing address of the corporation's principal office (it may be located outside of Wisconsin)
- a statement whether the corporation will have members or not
- name, address, and signature of each incorporator
- name of the person who drafted the document (printed, typewritten or stamped in a legible manner)

STATUTE: Wisconsin Statutes, Chapter 181

Wyoming

Corporations Division
Secretary of State
The Capital Building
Room 110
200 West 24th Street
Cheyenne, WY 82002-0020
307-777-7311

Website:
http://soswy.state.wy.us/corporat/
corporat.htm

LIMITED LIABILITY COMPANY

WHAT MUST BE FILED:

An original and one exact copy must be filed along with a written consent to appointment by the registered agent.

ARTICLES OF ORGANIZATION SPECIAL REQUIREMENTS:

The total of cash, a description, the agreed value of property other than cash contributed to the company, and any additional capital agreed to be contributed must be included in the Articles.

If there is a right to admit new members the terms of admission must be stated.

If the members have a right to continue the business after the termination of a member this must be stated.

The Articles must accompany a written consent by the registered agent to appointment as agent.

STATUTES:

Wyoming Statute beginning with 17-15-101.

CORPORATION

WHAT MUST BE FILED:

Complete the forms and file the original and one exact copy. The Articles must be accompanied by the written consent to appointment executed by the registered agent. Enclose the filing fee.

ARTICLES REQUIREMENTS:

The Articles must contain the following minimum:

- the corporate name
- a statement whether the corporation is a religious, a public benefit or a mutual benefit corporation
- the street address of your corporation's initial registered office and the name of the registered agent
- the name and address of each incorporator
- a statement whether your corporation shall have members
- provisions regarding the distribution of assets upon the dissolution of the corporation
- the date and signature of each incorporator

Do not forget to let your registered agent sign the "Consent to Appointment."

STATUTE: Wyoming Statute, Section 17-6-102

Appendix D:

State Departments of Revenue

This appendix contains contact information for the department of revenue of each state.

ALABAMA
Alabama Department of Revenue
50 North Ripley Street
Montgomery, AL 36132
334-242-1170
www.ador.state.al.us

ALASKA
Alaska Department of Revenue
P.O. Box 110400
333 West Willoughby
11th Floor SOB
Juneau, AK 99811
907-465-2300
www.revenue.state.ak.us

ARIZONA
Arizona Department of Revenue
P.O. Box 52138
Phoenix, AZ, 85072
602-255-3381
www.revenue.state.az.us

ARKANSAS
Arkansas Department of Finance and
  Administration
Office of State Revenue Administration
1900 West Seventh Street
Room 2062
Ragland Building
P.O. Box 1272
Little Rock, AR 72203
501-324-9052
www.state.ar.us/dfa

CALIFORNIA
California Franchise Tax Board (FTB)
Franchise Tax Board
P.O. Box 1468
Sacramento, CA 95812
Field Office
3321 Power Inn Road
Suite 250
Sacramento, CA 95826-3893
800-852-5711
www.ftb.ca.gov

California State Board of Equilization
450 N Street
Sacramento, CA
P.O. Box 942879
800-400-7115
www.boe.ca.gov

COLORADO

Colorado Department of Revenue
1375 Sherman Street
Denver, CO 80261
303-238-7378
www.revenue.state.co.us/main/
  home.asp

CONNECTICUT

State of Connecticut Department of
  Revenue Services
25 Sigourney Street
Hartford, CT 06106
800-382-9463
www.drs.state.ct.us

DELAWARE

State of Delaware Division of Revenue
Carvel Sate Office Building
820 North French Street
Wilmington, DE 19801
302-577-8200
revenue.delaware.gov

DISTRICT OF COLUMBIA

Office of the Chief Financial Officer
1350 Pennsylvania Avenue, North West
Suite 203
Washington, DC 20004
202-727-2476
cfo.dc.gov/cfo/site/default.asp

FLORIDA

Florida Department of Revenue
Taxpayer Services
Florida Department of Revenue
1379 Blountstown Highway
Tallahassee, FL 32304
800-352-3671
dor.myflorida.com/dor

GEORGIA

Georgia Department of Revenue
1800 Century Boulevard North East
Atlanta, GA 30345
404-417-4477
www.etax.dor.ga.gov

HAWAII

State of Hawaii Department of Taxation
P.O. Box 259
Honolulu, HI 96809
808-587-4242
www.state.hi.us/tax/tax.html

IDAHO

Idaho State Tax Commission
800 Park Boulevard
Plaza IV
Boise, ID 83712
800-972-7660
tax.idaho.gov/index.html

ILLINOIS

Illinois Department of Revenue
James R. Thompson Center
Concourse Level
100 West Randolph Street
Chicago, IL 60601
312-814-5232
www.revenue.state.il.us

INDIANA

Indiana Department of Revenue
Department of Revenue
100 North Senate Avenue
Indianapolis, IN 46204
317-233-4018
www.ai.org/dor/index.html

IOWA

Iowa Department of Revenue
Taxpayer Services
Iowa Department of Revenue
P.O. Box 10457
Des Moines, IA 50306
515-281-3114
www.state.ia.us/tax

KANSAS

Kansas Department of Revenue
915 SW Harrison Street
Tax Assistance
Docking State Office Building
Room 150
Topeka, KS 66612
785-368-8222
www.ksrevenue.org

LOUISIANA

Louisiana Department of Revenue
617 North Third Street
Baton Rouge, LA 70802
337-491-2504
www.rev.state.la.us

MAINE

Maine Revenue Services
24 State House Station
Augusta, ME 04333
287-2076
www.maine.gov/revenue

MARYLAND

Comptroller of Maryland
301 West Preston Street
Room 206
Baltimore, MD
410-260-7980
www.comp.state.md.us

MASSACHUSETTS

Massachusetts Department of Revenue
P.O. Box 7010
Boston, MA 02204
800-392-6089
www.dor.state.ma.us

MICHIGAN

Michigan Department of Treasury
Lansing, MI 48922
517-373-3200
www.michigan.gov/treasury

MINNESOTA

Minnesota Department of Revenue
600 North Robert Street
St. Paul, MN 55101
www.taxes.state.mn.us

MISSISSIPPI

Mississippi State Tax Commission
1577 Springridge Road
Raymond, MS 39154
601-923-7391
ww.mstc.state.ms.us

MISSOURI

Missouri Department of Revenue
Harry S. Truman State Office Building
301 West High Street
Jefferson City, MO 65101
573-751-4450
www.dor.mo.gov

MONTANA

State of Montana Department of
    Revenue
Sam W. Mitchell Building
125 North Roberts
3rd Floor
Helena, MT
406-444-6900
mt.gov/revenue

NEBRASKA

Nebraska Department of Revenue
Nebraska State Office Building
301 Centennial Mall South
P.O. Box 94818
Lincoln, NE 68509
800-742-7474
www.revenue.state.ne.us

NEVADA

Nevada Department of Taxation
Department of Taxation
1550 College Parkway
Suite 115
Carson City, NV 89706
775-684-2000
tax.state.nv.us

NEW HAMPSHIRE

New Hampshire Department of
    Revenue Administration
45 Chenell Drive
Concord, NH 03301
603-271-2191
www.nh.gov/revenue

NEW JERSEY

State of New Jersey Division of
    Taxation
Taxation Building
50 Barrack Street
1st Floor Lobby
Trenton, NJ 08695
609-292-6400
ww.state.nj.us/treasury/taxation

NEW MEXICO

State of New Mexico Taxation and
    Revenue
Taxation and Revenue Department
1100 South St. Francis Drive
P.O. Box 630
Santa Fe, NM 87504
505-827-0700
www.tax.state.nm.us

NEW YORK

New York State Department of
 Taxation and Finance
Manhattan District Office
1740 Broadway
New York, NY 10019
800-443-3200
www.tax.state.ny.us

NORTH CAROLINA

North Carolina Department of
 Revenue
P.O. Box 25000
Raleigh, NC 27640
877-252-3052
www.dor.state.nc.us

NORTH DAKOTA

North Dakota Office of State Tax
 Commissioner
600 E Boulevard Avenue
Dept. 127
Bismarck, ND 58505
701-328-2270
www.nd.gov/tax

OHIO

Ohio Department of Taxation
Tax Commissioners Office
30 East Broad Street
22nd Floor
Columbus, OH 43215
800-282-1780
tax.ohio.gov

OKLAHOMA

Oklahoma Tax Commission
2501 North Lincoln Boulevard
Oklahoma City, OK 73194
Connors Building
Capitol Complex
405-521-3160
www.oktax.state.ok.us

OREGON

Oregon Department of Revenue
955 Center Street North East
Salem, OR 97301
503-378-4988
www.oregon.gov/dor

PENNSYLVANIA

Pennsylvania Department of Revenue
Strawberry Square
Fourth and Walnut Street
Lobby
Harrisburg, PA 17128
717-783-6277
www.revenue.state.pa.us

RHODE ISLAND

Rhode Island Division of Taxation
One Capitol Hill
Providence, RI 02908
401-222-1040
www.tax.state.ri.us

SOUTH CAROLINA

South Carolina Department of
 Revenue
301 Gervais Street
P.O. Box 125
Columbia, SC 29214
803-898-5000
www.sctax.org/default.htm

SOUTH DAKOTA

South Dakota Department of Revenue and Regulation
445 East Capitol Avenue
Pierre, SD 58501
605-773-3311
www.state.sd.us/drr2/revenue.html

TENNESSEE

Tennessee Department of Revenue
Andrew Jackson Building
Room 1200
Nashville, TN 37242
800-342-1003
www.state.tn.us/revenue

TEXAS

Texas Department of Revenue
Susan Combs
Texas Comptroller
P.O. Box 13528
Capitol Station
Austin, TX 78711
800-248-4093
www.cpa.state.tx.us

UTAH

Utah State Tax Commission
210 North 1950 West
Salt Lake City, UT 84134
801-297-2200
tax.utah.gov/contact.html

VERMONT

Vermont Department of Taxes
133 State Street
Montpelier, VT 05633
802-828-2505
www.state.vt.us/tax

VIRGINIA

Virginia Department of Taxation
3610 West Broad
Richmond, VA 23230
804-367-8031
www.tax.virginia.gov

WASHINGTON

Washington State Department of Revenue
Taxpayer Account Administration
P.O. Box 47476
Olympia, WA 98504
800-647-7706
dor.wa.gov

WEST VIRGINIA

West Virginia State Tax Department
1206 Quarrier Street
Charleston, WV 25301
304-558-3333
www.state.wv.us/taxdiv

WISCONSIN

Wisconsin Department of Revenue
2135 Rimrock Road
Madison, WI 53713
608-267-0834
www.dor.state.wi.us

WYOMING

Wyoming Department of Revenue
Edmund J. Schmidt, Director
Herschler Building
2nd Floor West
Cheyenne, WY 82002
307-777-7961
revenue.state.wy.us

Index

About the Author

Mark Warda received his BA with Honors in Political Science from the University of Illinois in Chicago and his JD from the University of Illinois in Champaign. He also studied law at the university of Oxford, England and studied German in Cologne and Spanish in Barcelona.

Mark started his first business at the age of three when, after learning that one needs money to buy things, he started selling his drawings to visiting relatives. While practicing law he noticed that his clients had problems they would not have had if they had known something about the law before they came to him. So he started Sphinx Publishing to publish self-help law books. His first book was *Landlords' Rights and Duties in Florida* and his first printing sold out quickly. Over the next few years he wrote several more books and eventually quit practicing law to publish the books full time. After finding lawyers in other states interested in simplifying the law, he began publishing versions of his existing books adapted to those states.

By 1996 he found he was spending most of his time overseeing the publishing end of the business, so he sold the company to Sourcebooks to give himself more time to write books.

In 1998 he started Land Trust Service Corporation to service readers of his book *Land Trusts in Florida* who were looking for dependable, affordable trustee services.

Today Mark is continuing to update his collection of over sixty books and running Land Trust Service Corporation in Lake Wales, Florida with his wife, Alexandra, and his new son, Mark David.